Storey
BASICS®

P9-CBM-457

HOW TO KNIT SOCKS THAT FIT

Techniques for Toe-Up and Cuff-Down Styles

Donna Druchunas

Storey Publishing

*To knitters everywhere who have made the socks
that never cease to inspire me.*

---

*The mission of Storey Publishing is to serve our customers by
publishing practical information that encourages
personal independence in harmony with the environment.*

Edited by Gwen Steege and Kathy Brock
Series design by Alethea Morrison
Art direction by Michaela Jebb
Text production by Theresa Wiscovitch
Indexed by Nancy D. Wood

Cover illustration by © Fumi Koike
Interior illustrations by Alison Kolesar

© 2015 by Donna Druchunas

All rights reserved. No part of this book may be reproduced without written permission from the publisher, except by a reviewer who may quote brief passages or reproduce illustrations in a review with appropriate credits; nor may any part of this book be reproduced, stored in a retrieval system, or transmitted in any form or by any means — electronic, mechanical, photocopying, recording, or other — without written permission from the publisher.

The information in this book is true and complete to the best of our knowledge. All recommendations are made without guarantee on the part of the author or Storey Publishing. The author and publisher disclaim any liability in connection with the use of this information.

Storey books are available for special premium and promotional uses and for customized editions. For further information, please call 1-800-793-9396.

Storey Publishing
210 MASS MoCA Way
North Adams, MA 01247
www.storey.com

Printed in the United States by McNaughton & Gunn, Inc.
10 9 8 7 6 5 4 3 2 1

LIBRARY OF CONGRESS CATALOGING-IN-PUBLICATION DATA

Druchunas, Donna, author.
  How to knit socks that fit : techniques for toe-up and cuff-down styles / Donna Druchunas.
    pages cm. — (A Storey basics title)
  Includes index.
  ISBN 978-1-61212-541-1 (pbk. : alk. paper)
  ISBN 978-1-61212-542-8 (ebooks) 1. Socks. 2. Knitting—Technique. 3. Clothing and dress measurements. I. Title.
TT825.D746 2015
746.43'2—dc23
                              2015027119

CONTENTS

WHY KNIT SOCKS?

"Why do you knit socks?"

Almost everyone who knits socks has been asked this question. The next question, usually asked by a non-knitter with a furrowed brow and incredulous tone of voice, is, "Is it cheaper than buying them?"

Definitely not. These days you can buy socks for a few dollars a pair, quite a bit less than the cost of a skein of sock yarn. But the product you can buy for three dollars at your local discount store can't compare with the pair of socks you can make by hand, even with the least expensive sock yarn available.

Comfort is one reason to knit your own socks. There is nothing as comfortable and cozy as wearing a pair of handknit socks. Whether you choose warm wool for winter wear, heavy yarn for slippers, luxury sock yarn to wear while reading in bed, or cotton sock yarn for spring and summer (or Southern) wear, your handknit socks will be the most comfortable socks you have ever worn.

Socks are also a lot of fun to make. You can stick with a basic cuff-down (page 59) or toe-up (page 77) pattern if you want mindless knitting. Or if you're looking for a challenge, you can experiment with all different kinds of stitches and patterns on the leg and foot (see pages 107–118), you can try out different kinds of heel and toe techniques (see chapter 8), and you can play with solid, multicolored, and even self-striping yarns (see pages 9–10).

Commercial socks are sold in just a few sizes. For adults, stores typically carry just one "average" size for men and one for women. The choice isn't always straightforward, and you might not even be able to find socks that fit you properly. I wear a women's size 11 shoe (that's size 42 in Europe), so socks sold for women are usually too small for me, while socks sold for men are too big. When I make my own, they always fit just right.

Another reason to knit socks is to use the amazing sock yarns that are on the market today. Of course, you can use these yarns to make sweaters, shawls, and other accessories, but a sweater made of sock yarn, knit at 7 or 8 stitches per inch, could take a year to finish! Using sock yarn can be quite expensive for knitting shawls. And heavier yarns are often more practical for winter accessories like scarves, hats, and mittens. With just one skein of sock yarn (about 400 yards), you can make a whole pair of socks to fit an adult, or two pairs of kids' socks! And you can finish in a couple of weeks, or maybe even less.

Socks make wonderful gifts, too. Who would turn their nose up at a warm, comfy pair of socks? Whether showing them off in clogs (or sandals), wearing them inside winter hiking boots, or cuddling in front of the fire on a cold winter's evening, anyone who receives a present of handknit socks will appreciate the effort and love the gift.

Before you get started, I must warn you: knitting socks is addicting! Once you make your first pair, you'll be hooked, and before you know it, people will be asking *you*, "Why do you knit socks?" But with all of these benefits, the real question is, "Why *not* knit socks?"

CHAPTER ONE

YARN FOR KNITTING SOCKS

There are many different kinds of yarn that can be used for knitting socks. Not only are there different weights, or thicknesses, of yarns, but yarns are made from different fibers, dyed in both solid colors and multicolored patterns, and spun with different textures. Choosing the right yarn for your sock project is key to being happy with the end results.

YARN WEIGHTS

YARN THAT IS CALLED "SOCK YARN" by yarn manufacturers is usually fingering weight, also called 4-ply in the United Kingdom. The way yarns are categorized can be quite confusing, because even though there is a standard U.S. yarn weight system, most knitters use older names to describe the weight (which in this context refers to thickness, not actual weight), of yarn. The table below includes the Craft Yarn Council (CYC) standard yarn weight system, as well as common U.S. and U.K. names for the same yarns, along with gauge information, a suggested needle size range, and information about the types of socks that can

Standard Yarn Weights for Socks

CYC YARN WEIGHT	U.S. TERMS	U.K. TERMS	GAUGE (STITCHES PER 4")	NEEDLE SIZE RANGE U.S. SIZE (mm)	TYPES OF SOCKS
1	Fingering, sock, Baby	3- or 4-ply	27–32	1–3 (2.25–3.25 mm)	Socks to wear in close-fitting shoes
2	Sport, Baby	5-ply	23–26	3–5 (3.25–3.75 mm)	Socks for clogs or loose-fitting sneakers
3	DK, Light Worsted	8-ply	21–24	5–7 (3.75–4.5 mm)	Socks for clogs or hiking; work socks to wear in boots and slippers
4	Worsted, Aran	10- or 12-ply	16–20	7–9 (4.5–5.5 mm)	Hiking or work socks to wear in boots and slippers

This information is from the Craft Yarn Council Standard Yarn Weight System guidelines (www.craftyarncouncil.com).

be knit with each weight of yarn. While there are yarns that are both thinner and thicker than those I've listed here, I haven't used them for knitting socks.

FIBER CONTENT

IN ADDITION TO YARN WEIGHT, the fiber used to create a yarn is an important factor in the suitability of yarn for knitting socks. All yarns come from one of three sources: animals, plants, and chemistry (man-made materials).

Fibers from Animals

Protein, or animal-source, fibers make warm, breathable yarns that are easy to knit because the fibers have natural give, or stretch. Depending on the type of animal and specific breed, yarns from animal fibers can be soft enough to place next to a baby's skin or strong enough to wipe your feet on.

....

Using the Chart

The guidelines in the yarn-weights table on the facing page are based on my preferences and experience. If you check the CYC guidelines, you'll notice that they suggest both a looser gauge and larger needles for each yarn weight because the CYC guidelines are generic; my numbers are specifically for knitting socks. You may find patterns that are knit at different gauges than listed here, and you may need to use different needle sizes to get your desired gauge. (For more information about this, see pages 32–33.)

....

Wool is the most common animal fiber and comes from the fleece of sheep. Wool is warm and breathable and can absorb up to 30 percent of its weight in water without feeling wet, which makes it exceptionally practical for socks. Merino wool is the softest available and is quite popular in sock yarns; however, it is not the strongest of wool fibers for the same reasons it is soft: it has short, fine individual fibers. Merino sock yarns are almost always blended with nylon for added strength. Other breed-specific yarns such as Bluefaced Leicester, Polwarth, Romney, and others have become more popular of late and can now be found at fiber festivals, as well as online and at local yarn shops. Many sock yarns are made with wool from various meat- and fiber-sheep breeds, are often blended together, and do not list the specific breeds on the label.

Alpaca and llama fibers are spun into yarns that are similar to wool but have less elasticity. These yarns can be very soft, but they are usually denser and weigh more than wool yarns of the same thickness. These fibers are not as springy as wool, so the knitted fabric is not as stretchy, but they can be used successfully in combination with knitting stitches such as ribbing that add elasticity to the sock. When blended with wool, alpaca and llama make very warm socks for winter wear, as well as long-wearing hiking and work socks.

Cashmere yarn is made from the downy undercoat of Angora goats. This fiber, as well as other luxury fibers made from down fibers, such as qiviut (from the musk ox), bison, yak, and camel, are not strong enough for long-wearing socks but can be used for socks when blended with wool and nylon for strength.

Angora rabbit fur is the last fiber spun from the fur of a mammal that we'll discuss. While the pure fiber is deliciously soft and cuddly, the individual fibers are short and require a very tight twist (see page 10) to keep the yarn from shedding, even when blended with wool. A few high-twist angora-and-wool-blend yarns are on the market today, and these are excellent for extra-warm socks and slippers.

Silk is the only common protein fiber that does not come from the fleece of an animal. Silk comes from the fibers that form the cocoon of the *Bombyx mori* moth. The silkworm caterpillar spins a very strong fiber that can be made into yarn or fabric that is cool in summer and warm in winter. Because it has little elasticity, silk works best for socks only when blended with wool or another springy fiber.

Fibers from Plants

Cellulose, or plant-source, fibers usually have less elasticity than protein fibers and often make stronger yarns. Some are even used to make ropes.

Cotton is a versatile fiber that can be spun into a strong yarn. One of the most absorbent fibers available, cotton gains strength when wet, giving it a clear advantage for socks. Mercerized cotton is lustrous and inelastic, while unmercerized cotton is much more absorbent and softer. (Mercerization is a chemical treatment that gives the fibers strength and a lustrous finish, and also helps them take dye for vibrant, long-lasting colors.) Fabrics made from cotton tend to stretch out of shape as they get older. For scarves and shawls, this is not terribly important. Socks, however, will eventually lose their shape after many washings. Blending cotton with wool or a very small amount of spandex (a synthetic elastic fiber, such as Lycra) solves this problem. Using very fine cotton yarn with a very high twist for machine-made socks also solves this problem. This explains why many antique handknit socks, made from cotton yarn thin enough to be called a thread and knit at the astounding gauge of 10 to 20 stitches per inch, have held their shape over the years.

Linen, made from flax, is the oldest-known natural fiber. Linen is extremely strong and absorbent and, like cotton, was used to knit fine socks for summer wear in times past. Today's linen knitting yarns are not available at such fine weights and are too hard and inelastic for knitting socks unless blended with at least 50 percent wool.

Hemp and bamboo yarns have qualities very similar to linen.

Man-Made Fibers

As mentioned above, Lycra can be blended with cotton to add elasticity, and nylon or acrylic can be blended with wool to add strength and washability. Many other man-made fibers are practical for knitting socks as well. Although in the past synthetic fibers such as nylon and polyester were not absorbent or breathable, technologies are available today that make some new high-tech yarns that are much more appealing to sock knitters.

Still other fibers, such as Tencel, rayon, and some bamboo yarns, are made by chemical processes from plant material, becoming hybrids of the natural and man-made categories. Many of these yarns work well for socks when blended with wool, and you can often find them in the sock-yarn section of local yarn shops.

YARN COLORS

CHOOSING COLORS IS one of the most personal parts of knitting. In fact, most of the time when we look through books and magazines, the color of a project is what jumps out at us first. In this book, there is no color, so you get to exercise your imagination and choose what is best for you.

Solid colors are excellent choices for socks, especially if you're knitting for someone with conservative tastes. When the yarn is solid, it also shows up your pattern stitches with the best possible results. Solid colors can also be combined in colorwork patterns or stripes.

Semisolid colors are hand-dyed with slight variations. This gives you all of the advantages of working with solids and just a touch of added interest.

Ombré is a term that has come into popularity again lately. These yarns can also be called variegated or multicolored. Many times the colors blend into each other in a sequence that repeats one or more times in a skein. If you want to work a complicated stitch pattern in these yarns, swatch first to make sure the color pattern and stitch pattern don't compete with each other.

Self-striping and self-patterning yarns are clever color arrangements that create stripes or faux Fair Isle designs on your knitting without any extra work on your part. Working with these yarns is a fun way to add variety to your socks while keeping the knitting simple.

WHY TWIST AND SPIN MATTER

THE AMOUNT OF TWIST in the yarn and the technique used to spin it are of particular importance to sock knitters.

Yarns are made by spinning, which is essentially twisting individual fibers together. The shorter the fibers are, the more twist is required to hold them together, to prevent the yarn from pilling, and to make the yarn strong. The amount of twist also affects the elasticity of yarn. The looser the twist (or the fewer times the yarn is twisted per inch), the less elastic the resulting yarn will be. The tighter the twist (the more times the yarn is twisted per inch), the more spring and elasticity is added to the yarn.

Yarn that is spun with a *worsted* technique, where all of the fibers are arranged parallel to each other, is firm, dense, and strong. Yarn that is spun in the *woolen* technique, where fibers are arranged in a more haphazard fashion, is lofty and fluffy, with a lot of elasticity. (See also "Spinning Notes" on the facing page.)

Other factors, such as type of fiber and number of plies, also influence the amount of elasticity in a yarn. Yarn can be made from a single strand of spun fiber (referred to as *singles*) or from several strands that are plied (twisted) together. I don't consider singles yarns to be appropriate for knitting socks, although there are some singles sock yarns on the market. With just enough twist added (not too much or the yarn will kink up and bias when knit), a singles yarn can work for socks, but it will never have the elasticity or strength of a plied yarn. When multiple strands — two, three, four, or even more — of yarn are plied together, they create yarns of different textures, resulting in different amounts of elasticity, bounce, and strength.

....

Spinning Notes

Yarn can be spun either *worsted* (which refers to the spinning method rather than one of the yarn weights described above) or *woolen* style. Worsted yarns have the fibers all lined up in parallel to create a firm, strong yarn with a smooth surface that is wonderful for knitting cables and knit-and-purl patterns. Woolen yarn is spun from fibers that are jumbled in all different directions, which creates an elastic, fluffy yarn perfect for knitting colorwork patterns. Both styles of yarn work well for stockinette stitch and ribbing, and both are appropriate for knitting socks.

....

YARN AMOUNTS

THE TABLE BELOW gives a rough estimate of yardage required to knit socks based on calf-high socks in stockinette stitch or ribbing. Additional yarn will be needed for using complex stitch patterns and multiple colors. Many sock yarns today come in skeins of 400–500 yards, which is normally enough to make an adult-size pair of socks or two pairs of children's socks.

General Yardage Requirements for Socks

CYC YARN WEIGHT		CHILD'S SIZES (5"–8" FOOT LENGTH)	ADULT SIZES (9"–12" FOOT LENGTH)
1	Fingering, sock, Baby	150–275 yds	325–525 yds
2	Sport, Baby	125–225 yds	250–400 yds
3	DK, Light Worsted	125–200 yds	250–350 yds
4	Worsted, Aran	100–150 yds	175–275 yds

CHAPTER TWO

NEEDLES FOR KNITTING SOCKS

Socks, like everything else knitted, are made on knitting needles. My grandmother always used the same kind of needles, probably the only brand available at the discount store where she usually shopped for her yarn. Today, the variety of needles available to knitters is almost limitless. The downside to the available variety is that you have to choose!

NEEDLE MATERIALS

Wooden needles are smooth but not overly slippery and are a good choice for beginning sock knitters. Wooden needles are also warm, making them more comfortable to hold than other materials. The wood itself is often birch, but rosewood, ebony, and a variety of other woods may be used. The strength and flexibility of the needles varies based on the species of tree from which the wood is milled. I don't recommend using wooden needles at sizes smaller than U.S. 2 (2.75 mm) because they are prone to break unless you handle them gently.

Bamboo needles are stronger than wood, particularly in the smaller sizes, while providing the same advantages of being warm and smooth but not slippery.

Plastic needles are also warm and flexible and are another good choice for beginning sock knitters. They can be less expensive than wooden needles but are generally not available in the smallest sizes because of manufacturing limitations.

Metal needles are available in many different styles and brands today. In general, these make for fast knitting because they are slick and very smooth. They are also quite slippery, however, and can be frustrating for new sock knitters because they make it too easy to drop stitches, especially off the ends of double-pointed needles (more on that in the next section). Metal needles can be extremely slippery when nickel-plated, very slippery when made from stainless steel, and moderately slippery when coated or painted, but they are all more slippery than plastic, wooden, and bamboo needles. Very thin needles can be made with steel, however, making them popular for sock knitters who like to work with fine yarn and small needles to make firm, dense stitches and lightweight socks. These fine steel needles are flexible and will bend over time, however, which I find annoying.

Carbon-fiber needles are newcomers to the knitting marketplace. These needles are less slippery than metal needles and stronger than wood or bamboo, making them a new favorite of sock knitters. Some brands come with steel points on the ends of the needle for speedy knitting, while the carbon fiber of the needle shank holds stitches in place and helps reduce the frequency of dropping stitches.

KNITTING IN THE ROUND

SOCKS ARE KNIT CIRCULARLY, so they cannot be knit on two straight needles. Although it is possible to knit socks as flat pieces, then seam them together, the seams could be uncomfortable and also weaken the structure of the finished sock. There are several different techniques that can be used for knitting in the round, each requiring different types of knitting needles. These include:

- one short circular needle
- a set of four or five double-pointed needles
- two circular needles
- one long circular needle for a technique called "Magic Loop" (see page 21)

Let's look at how each of these works.

USING ONE SHORT CIRCULAR NEEDLE

The most obvious way to knit a small tube is to put the stitches on a short circular needle and work around and around and around. Some knitters are, in fact, quite fond of this method. Many other knitters find the short circulars difficult, if not impossible, to work with because the needle portion is only a few inches long, which, depending on how you hold your yarn and needles, makes it difficult to grasp.

- **Needle length:** 9 to 12 inches (must be shorter than the finished circumference of the sock)

1. Cast on the appropriate number of stitches, then place the needle on a flat surface, and make sure all the stitches are lined up on the inside of the needle's curve and not twisted. With the yarn tail and the working yarn on the right side of the needle, pick up the needle carefully, and knit the first couple of stitches with both strands. This joins the knitting into a circle. (When you come back to the beginning of the round, work the double-stranded stitches as single stitches.)

JOINING TO KNIT in the round on a short circular needle

2. Now just knit around and around and around. You can use the yarn tail to keep track of the beginning of the round (as I do), or you can put a little plastic marker onto the needle and slip it every time you come to it.

USING DOUBLE-POINTED NEEDLES

Double-pointed needles are straight needles that have points on both ends. By using four or five needles, it is possible to knit in the round without having a curved needle. This is the oldest way of knitting in the round and was used throughout the Middle East, Europe, and South America for centuries before circular needles were invented. You can put your work on three needles and knit with the fourth (common in the United States, this is my preference) or you can put your work on four needles and knit with the fifth (more common in Europe). If you've never used double-pointed needles before, try both setups to see which is most comfortable for you.

- **Needle length:** 5 to 8 inches

1. Cast on, then divide the stitches evenly onto three or four needles by just slipping the stitches from one needle to another.

2. Place the needles on a flat surface, and make sure all the stitches are lined up on the inside of the triangle or square formed by the needles and not twisted. With the tail and the working yarn on the right needle, pick up the needles carefully, and knit the first couple of stitches with both strands. This joins the knitting into a circle.

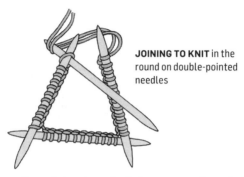

JOINING TO KNIT in the round on double-pointed needles

3. Drop the tail, and continue knitting across the stitches on the left needle with the working yarn, leaving the other needles hanging in the back of your work. Don't worry: As long as the stitches are not right near the tips of the needles, they won't fall out of the knitting.

4. After you knit across all the stitches on the left needle and it is empty, it becomes the new working needle. Rotate your work so the needle with the next unworked stitches is in your left hand and knit with the new working needle. Repeat this on each needle until you've worked all the stitches in the round, then continue with the next round.

Whenever you begin working on a new needle, hold the right needle *under* the needle to the right of the working needle to avoid a "ladder," or gap, where the two sections join.

USING TWO CIRCULAR NEEDLES

Because one short circular needle is difficult for many knitters to use and double-pointed needles seem fussy to others, two different ways of knitting small tubes on longer circular needles were introduced in the early 2000s. In the Summer 2000 issue of *Knitter's Magazine*, Joyce Williams introduced the concept of knitting on two circular needles to the knitting world. The popularity of Cat Bordhi's 2001 book *Socks Soar on Two Circular Needles: A Manual of Elegant Knitting Techniques and Patterns* (Passing Paws Press) ensured that this technique would become a standby for many new sock knitters.

- **Needle length:** 16 to 24 inches

1. Cast on the required number of stitches, then divide them evenly onto two circular needles so that the first needle holds the first half of the round and the second needle holds the second half of the round. Fold the stitches in half so the needle with the working yarn attached is in the back, with the yarn coming off the right edge of the knitting. Make sure the stitches are not twisted. One needle will be holding the stitches for the sole, and the other will be holding the stitches for the top of the foot. It generally does not matter which half is which until a pattern stitch is established on one part, making that the top of the foot.

(continued on next page)

2. To knit a round, using the first needle only, knit the first half of the round. Then pull the needle so the stitches just worked are on the cord between the two tips.

3. Turn the work around so the second half of the round is facing you. Switch to the second needle only to knit the second half of the round. The stitches always stay on the same needle.

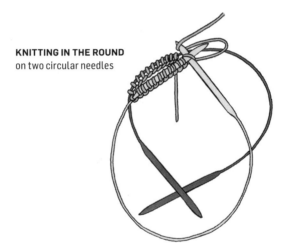

KNITTING IN THE ROUND
on two circular needles

Whenever you begin a new needle, pinch the cable of the unused needle close against the needle in your left hand to avoid a "ladder," or gap, where the two sections join.

USING ONE LONG CIRCULAR NEEDLE: THE MAGIC LOOP

The traditional way to knit on one circular needle is to use a needle that is slightly smaller in circumference than the piece you are knitting. If you're knitting a sweater in the round, this means you need needles ranging from 9 to 32 inches long, and even longer, plus, perhaps, double-pointed needles for cuffs. This can be quite expensive. Many knitters found ways to "cheat" and use a single long needle for knitting smaller tubes in the round. The technique we call "Magic Loop" was made popular in the 2002 book *The Magic Loop: Working Around on One Needle, Sara Hauschka's Magical Unvention*, by Bev Galeskas (Fiber Trends). This has become another standard knitting technique in the years since.

• **Needle length:** At least 29 inches (40 inches is preferred)

1. Put all the stitches onto one long circular needle. Count across half of your stitches, and pull the cable of the circular needle out between the two groups of stitches.

2. Hold the needles parallel with tips pointing to the right and the cable pulled out between the groups of stitches

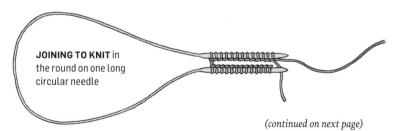

JOINING TO KNIT in the round on one long circular needle

(continued on next page)

and extending to the left. Push the stitches up onto the needles. The working yarn should be attached to the group of stitches on the back needle.

3. Pull the needle in the back out toward the right, sliding the stitches onto the cable, and use this needle to knit across the stitches on the front needle. There will now be a cable loop on both sides of the knitting.

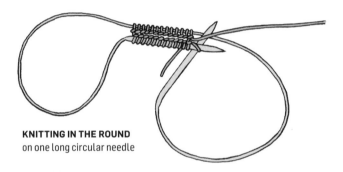

KNITTING IN THE ROUND
on one long circular needle

4. When you have worked across all the stitches in the front, turn the work around and repeat steps 2 and 3.

Whenever you begin a new section with this method, pinch the cable of the unused needle close against the needle in your left hand to avoid a "ladder," or gap, where the two sections join.

TIPS FOR ARRANGING STITCHES ON DIFFERENT KINDS OF NEEDLES

As you work on your sock, you will need to rearrange the stitches on the needles for several parts of the project to make the work easier to manage. The setup is different depending on whether you are working on double-pointed or circular needles.

DOUBLE-POINTED NEEDLES

- **Cuff and leg:** Divide stitches into three or four equal sections (or *almost* equal if necessary to keep full repeats on each needle).
- **Heel:** Put the heel stitches on one needle, and divide the remaining stitches equally on two needles to be worked later.
- **Gusset shaping:** Divide the sole (including the gusset stitches picked up on each side of the heel) on two needles; the end of the round should be in the center of these two needles. Put the instep stitches on one or two needles; you

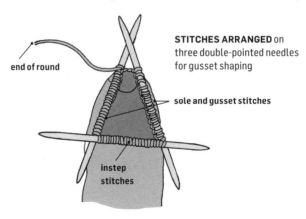

end of round

STITCHES ARRANGED on three double-pointed needles for gusset shaping

sole and gusset stitches

instep stitches

will work gusset decreases on each of the sole needles on the ends farthest away from the center of the heel.

- **Foot and toe:** Keep the instep on one or two needles and the sole divided equally on two needles.

TWO CIRCULAR NEEDLES OR MAGIC LOOP

- **Cuff and leg:** Divide the stitches in half, with the back of the leg on one needle or section and the front of the leg on the second needle or section.
- **Heel:** Put the heel stitches on one needle or section and the remaining stitches on the other needle or section to be worked later.

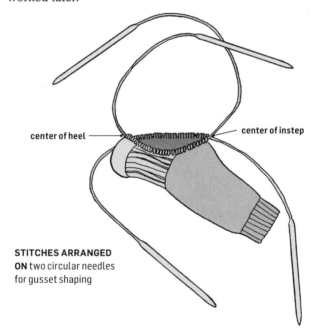

center of heel

center of instep

STITCHES ARRANGED ON two circular needles for gusset shaping

- **Gusset shaping:** Beginning at the center of the heel, put half of the stitches (up to the center of the instep) on one needle or section and the second half of the stitches (from the center of the instep to the center of the heel) on the second needle or section, placing markers between the sole and instep on each side; you will work gusset decreases in the middle of each section.
- **Foot and toe:** Divide the stitches in half, placing the sole stitches on one needle or section and the instep stitches on the second needle or section.

ONE SHORT CIRCULAR NEEDLE

If you're working on one short circular needle, there's no trick. All the stitches flow around the needle automatically. When working the heel, put the unworked stitches on scrap yarn or leave them on the needle while working back and forth on the heel stitches only.

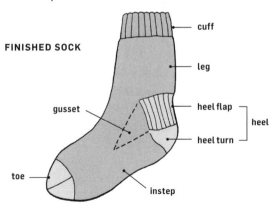

FINISHED SOCK

cuff

leg

gusset

heel flap

heel

heel turn

toe

instep

CHAPTER THREE

SOCK FIT AND SIZING

Knitting socks is fun, but it also takes a lot of time, so we want to be sure that the socks we make by hand fit the way we intend. This takes a little bit of forethought and may not be completely intuitive.

When you want to be sure your beautiful handknit socks will fit, you have two main considerations: (1) how big are the feet you're making the socks for, and (2) what needle size will give you the correct number of stitches per inch with the yarn you are using, thereby ensuring that the socks come out the right size. For the first, you need to take measurements; for the second, you need to make a gauge swatch.

TAKING FOOT MEASUREMENTS

THE KEY MEASUREMENTS for sock sizing are the ankle and foot circumferences. Most women's sock patterns are written to knit up at about 8 inches around; for men, it's about 10 inches. These average sizes provide a good fit for many people, but in actuality, our ankles are all different circumferences. If you want to get a really comfortable fit, therefore, it's smart to find the correct measurements. Refer to Measuring Your Foot on page 28 to find out just how to get them.

Once you have these key measurements, you must adjust them to account for what is called *negative ease*; that is, the measurements of the finished socks should be slightly smaller than the measurements of the feet the socks are meant to fit. (The term is used for other garments as well.) For stretchy knitting (stockinette stitch and lace, for instance), the sock should measure about 10 percent less than the size of the foot; for colorwork, 5 percent. If you're knitting ribbing, the fabric is so stretchy, you can make a sock that is 25 percent less than your foot measurement and it will still fit. This makes ribbing an especially good pattern-stitch choice for knitting socks for gifts.

You can simply estimate 1 inch of negative ease when knitting for adults and ½ inch when knitting for kids or doing colorwork. Your socks should hug your foot snugly but not be so tight as to pinch or stretch out of shape when worn. Some people even prefer to have some wiggle room for their toes. Remember, too, that the sock leg and ankle need to be stretchy enough to fit over your heel.

Measuring Your Foot

WHAT TO MEASURE	HOW TO MEASURE	YOUR MEASUREMENT
Foot Circumference	Loosely wrap a tape measure around the widest point of your foot.	_____ inches
Ankle Circumference	Loosely wrap a tape measure around your ankle just above the ankle bone.	_____ inches
Foot Length	While standing, measure from the back of your heel to the tip of your longest toe. This is easiest if you stand on a ruler or tape measure.	_____ inches
Leg Length	While standing, measure from the floor to the point on your leg where you want the top of the sock cuff to fall.	_____ inches

FOOT MEASUREMENTS

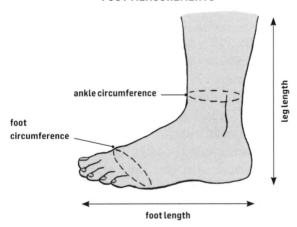

A caveat about negative ease: Subtracting from the measurements assumes that you are knitting with typical sock yarn and that you are not doing stranded colorwork. If you are knitting with a much thicker yarn, do not subtract as much from the ankle measurement. If you're knitting in colorwork, which is much less stretchy than single-color knitting, you'll need your sock to be a little bigger. Remember, if you're knitting k1, p1 or k2, p2 ribbing (see page 109), you almost can't make a sock too small.

Tips for Getting a Good Fit

- When making a sock with negative ease, remember that stretching it wider will make it shorter! So if you make a sock that is quite a bit smaller in circumference than your foot, you may need to add a little extra length so it doesn't pull tightly at the tip of your toes.

- Plain stockinette stitch on the sole, heel, and top of the foot has less bulk and may make a sock fit better in your shoes.

- Ribbing is very stretchy, so it is good to use on the leg and perhaps on top of the foot to ensure a good fit, especially for making socks as a gift (when you can't measure or try the socks on for fit).

- When making socks for gifts, adding a long cuff of ribbing allows the recipient to fold down the cuff for a custom leg length.

WORKING A GAUGE SWATCH

IN ADDITION TO MEASURING YOUR FOOT (or feet if they are not the same size, which you will already know), you also need to measure the gauge of your knitting. Don't whine. If you want socks that come out the right size, you absolutely do need to make a gauge swatch. Better still, work the swatch in the round rather than flat, since that's how the sock will be knit.

When working with a yarn not originally meant for socks, use needles a size or two smaller than the ball band calls for. Socks are knit at a tighter gauge than other garments to maximize wear. You'll find that they feel better on your feet that way, too.

To make your swatch, cast on enough stitches to work in the round (at least 36 stitches) and in a multiple of the number of stitches required for your pattern stitch. (For example, if your pattern stitch indicates that it is a multiple of 8 stitches, cast on 32 or 40 stitches, depending on what type of stitch you're using.) Join to work in the round, being careful not to twist the stitches, and work several repeats of your pattern; you should have at least 3 to 4 inches of knitting.

Sometimes different parts of a sock have different gauges and different pattern stitches. You need to get the right gauge for each part of the sock for it to fit right, which may require using a different needle size for each part. I definitely (let's be honest!) would never knit two gauge swatches for a project. Instead, I would put a lifeline (see facing page) in after I finished a section that came out just the way I wanted, then proceed with the needle size I think will work for the next section. If it isn't right, I can always rip back to the lifeline and try a different size.

Lifelines

A lifeline can be a lifesaver in knitting! It is simply a piece of string or yarn that is pulled through all of the stitches on the needles. Whenever you reach a point in your knitting where you are very happy with the results so far, and you are ready to start another pattern repeat or a different section of the sock, you can place a lifeline. This will give you the assurance that even if you mess up and have to rip out the knitting that comes next, the part you've already completed is safe.

To add a lifeline, thread a piece of string or yarn that is thinner than your working yarn onto a tapestry needle; I suggest cotton yarn, sewing thread, or unwaxed dental floss. Draw the needle through all the stitches on the knitting needles, being sure *not* to draw it through any stitch markers. Remove the tapestry needle and tie the ends of the lifeline string together. Later if you have to rip, you can remove your needles and rip out the knitting down to the lifeline, and all your stitches will be secure and in the correct orientation to place back on the needles. If you have trouble getting the stitches back on the working needles, put them onto smaller needles first, then continue knitting with the correct size needles for your project.

Measuring the Swatch

Stitch gauge is important in almost all knitting projects. If your stitch gauge is not exact, your socks will not come out the size indicated in the pattern.

To measure the stitch gauge, place a ruler or tape measure across your swatch horizontally. With pins, mark the beginning and end of 4 inches, and count the stitches between the pins. (Because your gauge may vary over the knitted piece, measuring over 4 inches gives a more accurate result.) When you measure ribbing, stretch the fabric slightly.

Divide by 4 to calculate the number of stitches per inch. Check the recommended gauge for your pattern. If your swatch has more stitches per inch than recommended, your stitches are too tight; try again with a larger needle. If it has fewer stitches per inch than recommended, your stitches are too loose; try again with a smaller needle.

To measure row gauge, place the ruler across the swatch vertically, mark 4 inches with pins, and count the rows.

Sometimes it's easy to think our gauge is "close enough," but if you're a stitch per inch or even a fraction of a stitch per inch off in your gauge measurements, the socks you are making will not come out the size specified in the pattern. For example, if a pattern calls for 9 stitches per inch and you get 8 stitches per inch, with 80 stitches in a sock, that's the difference between an 8¾-inch circumference and a 10-inch circumference — not even close to the correct size! Even if the difference in gauge is as little as ¼ stitch per inch (or 1 stitch per 4 inches), it can add up to an inch or more around an entire sock. (The variance will be slightly less if you're making socks at a looser gauge with around 60 or 70 stitches for your size, but it still makes a substantial difference.)

Keep notes about your measurements and stitch counts on the first sock, as suggested below, especially if you make any changes, so you can make the second sock the same.

Remember that getting gauge is 10,000 times more important than using the same size needles listed in the pattern! In fact, I could say it's *infinitely* more important because using the same needle size listed in the pattern is of zero importance. Even when you have faithfully knit your swatch, however, you still need to be ready to tweak as you go, because our knitting tension can change with our mood, and for many knitters, gauge loosens up as they relax into a project.

Recording Your Swatch Information

Yarn	_____	
Pattern Stitch	_____	
Needle Size Used for Swatch	_____	U.S. size / mm
Stitch Gauge	_____	stitches per 4"
Row Gauge	_____	rows per 4"

It's Okay to Cheat (Just a Little)

Here are a couple of ways to shortcut your swatching:

- **Work a flat swatch, instead of circular.** If you really don't want to make a swatch in the round, you can cheat and knit your swatch flat on double-pointed or circular needles. Here's how: As above, cast on at least 36 stitches (adjusting as necessary to get the right multiple of stitches for your pattern stitch). *Work across the row in pattern. Do not turn. Slide the knitting to the other end of the needle and *very loosely* draw the working yarn across the back of the work. Repeat from * until you've completed several repeats of your pattern, working until you have at least 3 to 4 inches of knitting.

- **Go straight to the sock.** Instead of knitting a swatch, you can cast on and use the cuff (or toe if it happens to be toe-up) as your gauge swatch. So if you get the cuff or toe done and the gauge is correct, then voilà, you're ahead of the game! If, however, the gauge is not right, you do have to rip out and start over. Don't just keep going if your gauge is off. If you're getting too few stitches per inch, for instance, you'll end up wasting time on knitting a sock for Bigfoot. Or if you have too many stitches per inch (although I find that much less common), you'll have to look for a kid to wear them.

CHOOSING WHAT SIZE TO MAKE

WITH THESE TWO GAUGE measurements (row and stitch), along with your foot measurements, you can figure out approximately how many stitches you need to cast on to knit your sock. An approximate number is just fine because you'll be following a pattern, so this number helps you find the pattern size that is closest to the fit that you desire. Remember, too, that the number of stitches you cast on will also be determined somewhat by the ribbing you want to do. K1, p1 rib requires an even number of stitches; k2, p2 rib requires that the number of stitches be divisible by 4. If you're doing a pattern stitch on the sock leg, you must account for the stitch multiple of the pattern as well.

When you calculate the number of stitches you need for the circumference of your sock, if your foot and ankle are not the same circumference, use your ankle measurement for cuff-down socks and your foot measurement for toe-up socks, because those are the parts you will knit first. You can make adjustments before or after the heel, if necessary, to accommodate different ankle and foot circumferences. Unless the difference is drastic, you won't need to make any adjustments at all, because knitted fabric is stretchy. (See Making Adjustments as You Knit, page 37, for more tips on customizing sock fit.)

Finding out how many stitches you need for the circumference of your sock requires a little arithmetic. Don't panic; it's no more math than you need to halve or double a recipe! Here's an example: If your yarn provides a gauge of 30 stitches over 4 inches, divide by 4 to get the number of stitches to the inch

(7½ stitches). Then multiply this number by the ankle/foot circumference less 1 inch (for single-color socks). So here's the math for someone with an 8-inch ankle who wants a 7-inch sock (note that result is rounded down; see below):

$$7\frac{1}{2} \text{ stitches per inch} \times 7 \text{ inches} = 52 \text{ stitches}$$

Use the following formula to calculate your own stitch count.

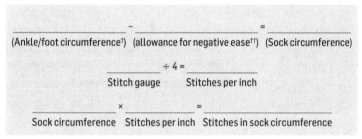

______	−	______	=	______
(Ankle/foot circumference†)		(allowance for negative ease††)		(Sock circumference)
______	÷ 4 =	______		
Stitch gauge		Stitches per inch		
______	×	______	=	______
Sock circumference		Stitches per inch		Stitches in sock circumference

†Ankle for cuff-down socks; foot for toe-up socks

††1" for adults; ½" for children and colorwork

Choose the size in the pattern that has the number of stitches in the cast on closest to the result you got when you calculated your stitch count. The patterns in this book are worked in ribbing stitches for maximum elasticity, but you will undoubtedly encounter patterns made with other stitches, so here's what to keep in mind:

- If it's stretchy, like lace or ribbing, choose the next smaller size.
- If it's not stretchy, like colorwork, slip-stitch patterns, or dense cables, choose the next larger size.

The biggest variation among sizes is foot length, but don't worry about that when you're selecting the size to knit. You can knit most socks to the desired length, and you can also try them on as you go. In fact, I recommend that the best way to ensure a good fit is: Try it on. Try it on. Try it on! Also, check gauge often, and change needle size if your gauge changes.

Making Adjustments as You Knit

- The base of the heel flap will sit at the base of your physical heel. The heel turn is what goes around the curve of your heel. A heel flap lets you adjust the instep depth. For an average instep, use a square heel flap. For a high instep, make the heel flap taller than wide. For a shallower instep, make the heel flap wider than tall. (See pages 41 and 53 for information about heel flaps.)

- The circumference is measured *inside* the sock. And remember that the fabric has thickness. This is particularly important when making thick socks.

- Most toe-shaping techniques result in a toe that is approximately 2 inches long on a medium-size adult sock. You can change the toe length as you knit by adjusting the spacing of increases (for toe up) or decreases (for cuff down).

- If your foot is bigger around than your ankle, when decreasing for the gusset, leave more stitches for the instep than for the ankle. (This is much more difficult to maneuver on toe-up socks!)

Shoe Sizes

If you're making socks for yourself or a family member, trying the socks on as you go is the best way to make sure they come out the right size. If you're making socks for a gift, that's not always possible, so working from a shoe-size chart is the next best thing.

Children's Sizes

SHOE SIZE (U.S.)	0–4	4–8	7–11	10–2	2–6
Age	6–12 months	1–3 years	3–5 years	5–9 years	7–13 years
Foot Circumference	4½"	5½"	6"	6½"	7"
Foot Length	4"	5"	6"	7½"	8"
Sock Length	2½"	3½"	4½"	5½"	6½"

Women's Sizes

SHOE SIZE (U.S.)	3–6	6–9	10–12
Sock Size (U.S.)	S (7–9)	M (9–11)	L (10–12)
Foot Circumference	7"	8"	9"
Foot Length	9"	10"	11"
Sock Length	6½"	7"	7½"

Men's Sizes

SHOE SIZE (U.S.)	6–8	8½–10	10½–12	12½–14
Sock Size (U.S.)	S (10)	M (11)	L (12)	XL (14)
Foot Circumference	7"	8"	9"	10"
Foot Length	9½"	10½"	11"	11½"
Sock Length	7"	7½"	8"	8½"

The information in these charts is from the Craft Yarn Council Standard Body Measurements/Sizing guidelines.

CHAPTER FOUR

THE PARTS OF A SOCK

Whether you knit a sock starting at the top of the cuff or at the tip of the toe, you'll find the same basic sections in almost all sock patterns. A few years ago, I would have said this was true of all sock patterns, but today there are some really creative sock knitters out there who are doing things outside the box. I prefer to stick with the traditional time-honored shapes and techniques that can easily be scaled for any size and adapted for many different kinds of pattern stitches.

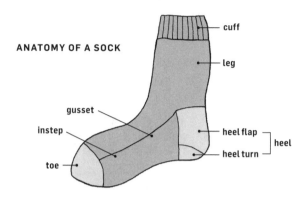

ANATOMY OF A SOCK

cuff
leg
gusset
instep
heel flap
heel
heel turn
toe

The Cuff

This is the part of the sock at the top edge. It is what holds the sock up, so it needs to be both snug and elastic. Many times this is knit in ribbing to provide both of those qualities. But many older socks and stockings (the old-time name for kneesocks) were knit plain all the way to the top and held up with garters — not the elastic kind we think of today, but ribbons or other ties that were either woven through eyelets near the top of the cuff or just wrapped around the outside of the sock and tied in a knot or bow.

The Leg

For shorter socks, the leg is just a straight tube. All of the patterns in this book are knit calf high with straight legs.

The Heel

The heel is the most complicated part of a sock because it needs to make a 90-degree turn. The heel is also the part of the sock that controls the depth of the instep. Almost all heels can be looked at as two parts: a heel flap, or a flat part of the heel that is worked on the back of the sock attached to the bottom of the leg, and a heel turn, or the part of the heel that turns the corner. Some sock heels have both elements, but others — such as most short-row heels (see pages 89–93) and the afterthought heel (see page 93) — consist only of a big heel turn. We'll talk about the details more in later sections, so don't worry if you aren't yet familiar with those types of heels.

- **The heel flap** is basically just a rectangle knit back and forth on the back of the leg. On socks that have one, the length of the heel flap controls the depth of the instep: a longer heel flap results in a deeper instep, and a shorter heel flap results in a shallower instep.

- **The heel turn** is where you make that 90-degree corner at the back of the sock while, at the same time, making a bump that sticks out from the tube of the sock for your heel. This can be worked in many different ways, almost all of which include working short rows (rows where you turn before the end), decreases, or some combination of the two. This can be the most complex and confusing part of the sock for knitters, and it's difficult to envision before you actually work it on the needles because you are building a three-dimensional shape out of a one-dimensional piece of string. But once you knit a sock and see how it works on your own needles, it'll make perfect sense.

The Gusset

Gussets are worked whenever you have a heel flap. The gusset shaping allows you to have extra stitches in your sock around the heel and instep area. The gusset section of the sock is where you either remove these extra stitches (cuff down) or add them (toe up). It is worked with simple decreases or increases.

The Foot

The main part of the foot of a sock is a straight tube. Sometimes a pattern stitch is worked on the top of the foot. Stockinette stitch is always worked on the sole. In colorwork socks, the sole often has a pattern that is very simple and easy to work, while the top of the foot typically has a more complicated and ornate pattern.

The Toe

The toe is usually worked with decreases (in cuff-down socks) or increases (in toe-up socks); the exception is when it is worked with short rows. What's great about short-row toes is that you can work them exactly the same way as short-row heels and — because the knitted fabric is stretchy — the heel makes a 90-degree turn and the toe folds over and almost closes on itself like a clam shell.

Knitting Kneesocks

For kneesocks (or even longer stockings), the leg is wider at the top and narrower at the ankle, requiring a change in needle size, pattern stitch, number of stitches, or some combination of all three. Decreases or increases for shaping the leg can be made around a center-back faux-seam stitch or worked into the patterning for a decorative effect. (See also Shaping Kneesocks, page 52.)

CHAPTER FIVE

CUFF DOWN OR TOE UP?

There are two basic ways to knit a sock: starting at the cuff and working down toward the toe, and starting at the toe and working up toward the cuff. I think cuff-down socks are easier to fit, so for your first pair of socks you might choose that approach, using a heel flap (see page 61) and wedge toe (see page 66). Both techniques have die-hard fans, and neither technique is inherently better than the other. The origins of these two opposite ways to knit socks lie far away and back in time.

A LITTLE HISTORY

TOE-UP SOCKS WERE TRADITIONALLY made in southern and eastern regions of the Old World, specifically in southern Europe and, even earlier, in the Middle East. In this part of the world, shoes were loose fitting and often made from leather with no firm sole. Shoes were not worn indoors, and people often sat on the floor, so socks were made with decorative stitches on the foot and sole as well as on the leg. In some places, people wore two pairs of socks: plain or textured white socks and colorwork outer socks, which gave added cushioning inside of shoes and also doubled as slippers when in the house. Because shoes were loose fitting, socks were also made with extra ease to fit loosely. And with elaborate colorwork patterning on the foot and leg, the extra size made it easy to put the socks on even though the fabric was not stretchy.

Cuff-down socks were traditionally made in northern and western Europe. In this part of the world, shoes often fit more snugly than in the south and east. Because the climate was colder in most cases, shoes were also made of sturdier materials and — where people could afford it — with heavy, solid soles. Socks were made to fit more snugly inside these fitted shoes. The upper classes wore elaborately styled shoes with finely knit socks made of silk or cotton, knit at up to 20 stitches per inch.

STRUCTURAL DIFFERENCES

It's not only the history of cuff-down and toe-up socks that makes them different. The way the heels and toes are constructed traditionally resulted in socks that fit and looked different even when they were not being worn. Although with modern yarns, tools, and techniques both cuff-down and toe-up socks can be made to fit any foot, each structure lends itself more easily to a certain kind of fit and function.

Today's patterns are adapted so both cuff-down and toe-up socks can be made with the same comfortable fit for modern shoes. Knitting socks with different types of yarns and at different gauges can provide options for knitting socks to wear in dress shoes, casual shoes and sneakers, under boots, or even as slippers. So how do you decide which to make?

PROS AND CONS

Since the historical distinctions don't exist today (loose-fitting shoes versus hard soles, for example), you might wonder what the advantages and disadvantages of each type of sock are. Here's a general rundown of the pros and cons as I see them.

Cuff-Down Socks
- For beginners, cuff-down socks are easier to make because they start with the straight leg and a relatively easy cast-on process.
- The toe on cuff-down socks is easier to replace if it wears out or develops a hole.

- It's easier to adjust for a very high or very shallow instep on cuff-down socks made with a heel that has a flap and turn.
- It's easier to change the length of the foot on a cuff-down sock because you can try it on just before you knit the toe and change the rate of decrease for toe shaping as you go.
- Cuff-down sock toes are often grafted with Kitchener stitch (see page 68). What can I say? You love it or hate it.

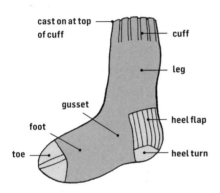

cast on at top of cuff

cuff

leg

gusset

foot

heel flap

toe

heel turn

CUFF-DOWN SOCKS naturally lie flat with the heel sticking out to the side. The end of the round is at the center bottom of the foot. The end of the round on the leg can be at the center back or on the side, and this can be decided when you begin working the heel.

Toe-Up Socks

- For experienced knitters, toe-up socks provide a new challenge.
- Toe-up socks allow you to use up every spare drop of yarn, especially if you knit two socks at once (see page 104).
- Some knitters find it easier to try on toe-up socks as they go.
- It's easier to change the length of the leg on toe-up socks because you can try it on before and after you knit the cuff and easily add or remove a few rows.

- It's easier to get a very stretchy edge at the top of the cuff on toe-up socks by working a stretchy bind off.

In the end, try both techniques and see what you find the most enjoyable to knit. If you like to have small knitting projects to take on the road or to places where you knit in public, you'll find that you can memorize your favorite techniques and pattern and knit socks as a mindless project after making just a few pairs.

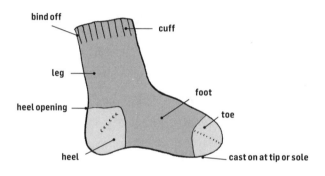

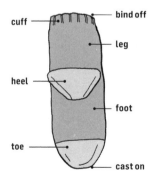

TOE-UP SOCKS naturally lie flat with the heel flush against the leg when folded down. The end of the round is at the side edge of the foot and the side of the leg.

CHAPTER SIX

KNITTING CUFF-DOWN SOCKS

Now let's go through the parts of a cuff-down sock in more detail, working from the cast-on edge at the top of the cuff and working our way down to the toe. This is an overview, so don't worry if some parts seem confusing. I'll go over each part in even more detail again when we are knitting.

You want a loose cast on for cuff-down socks, because the cast on has to stretch over your heel and fit comfortably on your leg without binding, so let's start with that.

Choosing the Best Cast On and Cuff

I use a long-tail cast on (see page 50) for my socks, and I've never had a problem with it. I usually work it over two needles held together, and although that doesn't actually make the cast-on edge stretchier, it does make the stitches in the first row larger, which means the first round of knitting on double-pointed needles is a lot easier to knit. The same result can be achieved by casting on with a larger needle.

CASTING ON for a cuff-down sock

Usually I work some kind of ribbing for a cuff. This provides extra elasticity and stretch.

KNITTING A CUFF for a cuff-down sock

The Loose Long-Tail Cast On

If you normally work the long-tail cast on with a slip knot, try this technique instead so you won't have a knot in the top edge of your sock. For the "long tail," pull out about 1 inch of yarn per stitch.

1. Hold the needle in your right hand and drape the long tail of yarn over the top of the needle so the tail is away from you (in the back) and the working yarn attached to the ball is near you (in 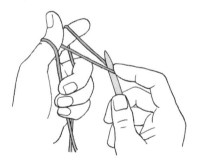 the front). Cross the strands underneath the needles. This forms the first stitch, which at this point is just an unsecured loop around the needles.

2. With the tail of the yarn over your left thumb and the working yarn over your index finger, pull the strands open. Grasp the strands in your palm and pull the needle down so that the yarn forms a V between your thumb and index finger.

3. Make each stitch by inserting the needle into the loop on your thumb from bottom to top. Bring the needle around the strand of yarn on your index finger from right to left, and catch the yarn on the needle. Pull the yarn back through the loop on your thumb from top to bottom.

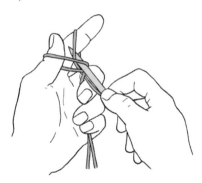

4. Pull your thumb out of the loop. You now have another stitch on the needle. Push the stitches away from the tip of the needle so the next stitch you make won't be smooshed right up next to the existing stitches. This will create extra yarn between stitches and make the edge stretchier.

5. Reposition your thumb under the tail, and tug gently to tighten the new stitch on the needle. Do not let go of the strands held in your palm.

Repeat steps 1–5 until you have the required number of stitches on the needle.

Straight or Shaped Legs

On a cuff-down sock, you either knit the leg straight or, for a kneesock, decrease as you go down toward the ankle.

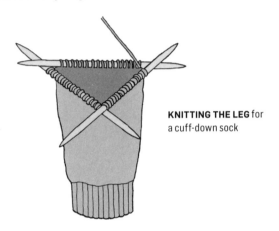

KNITTING THE LEG for a cuff-down sock

Shaping Kneesocks

The socks in this book are all calf length with straight legs. For kneesocks, you can work decreases into the pattern in any way you like for decorative effects. Another way to shape kneesocks is to decrease on each side of a center-back stitch, just as you would do for a sleeve on a seamless top-down sweater. I've also made kneesocks without shaping by decreasing; instead, I changed my needle size and pattern stitches for different parts of the leg to create the various circumferences at the cuff, calf, and ankle.

Turning the Heel

You can work any type of heel you want on a cuff-down sock. I usually do socks with flaps and turns, as explained here.

A heel flap is just a rectangle worked on half the stitches in the sock — plus or minus a stitch if you want to center the pattern on the heel a certain way. You can work it in plain stockinette stitch, put garter stitch on the side edges, or use heel stitch, where you slip every other stitch on right-side rows (see pages 61–62). Usually you slip the first stitch of every row to create a chain edge up the side of the sock, where each edge stitch is actually stretched out over 2 rows of knitting.

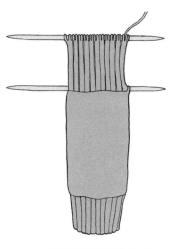

KNITTING A HEEL FLAP
on a cuff-down sock

This makes it very easy to pick up stitches on the sides of the heel flap later, which is what you have to do to get back to knitting in the round for the foot.

The heel turn is what makes the heel into a little box that turns the 90-degree angle from leg to foot. Some heel turns are quite rectangular, while others are more curved. The rectangular ones work only because knitting is stretchy and the soft fabric will mold itself to your foot. The curved ones are a little bit harder to keep track of when you're knitting, but many people prefer the fit. (The oldest heels were made simply by knitting a big heel flap, folding it in half, and seaming it on the bottom with a three-needle bind off! How does that sound for comfort?) A heel turn is worked on a few stitches at the center of the heel flap, and stitches at the end of each row are joined to the unused stitches from the heel flap with decreases. In the illustration on page 87, you can see the French heel,

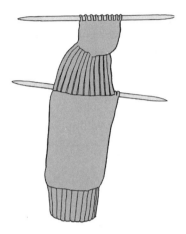

KNITTING A HEEL TURN
for a cuff-down sock

which has a flap with curves worked into it because, as you work the flap, each row is a little longer than the previous row. The sock in the illustration above has a Dutch heel, which is a true rectangle.

Heel Variations

Sometimes I work a short-row heel (see page 74) for variety. I almost never do an afterthought heel (see page 93) unless I want to do a heel with colorwork; in that case, the afterthought heel allows me to knit in the round.

Onto the Final Lap: The Foot

So what happens after you knit the heel? You started your sock working in the round, then you knit the heel back and forth. When the heel is done, you need to get back to working in the round again.

If you did a short-row heel (page 74), that's easy! You just knit all the way around on all of the stitches, and you're back to the tube for the foot. Because the short-row heel doesn't have a heel flap, it doesn't create an awkward shape that blocks you from going all the way around.

With a heel flap, after you turn the heel, you'll notice that you have two sets of stitches (the heel stitches and the others that you set aside while you worked on the heel). These two sets are separated by the rest of the heel, with the sides of the heel sitting there in between the two groups of live stitches. In order to have all the stitches next to each other and begin to knit in a tube again, you have to pick up and knit stitches on both sides of the heel flap.

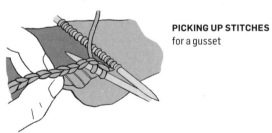

PICKING UP STITCHES
for a gusset

You'll now notice another surprise: You have more stitches than you started with! After turning the heel, you don't have as many stitches as you did at the beginning of the heel; however, after you pick up the stitches on the sides of the flap, you will have more than you first cast on. So you have to decrease at both sides of the foot until you are back to your original number. This is called *gusset shaping* (or sometimes you may see it called *instep shaping*).

After that, the rest of the sock is easy-peasy because you knit the foot without shaping, then decrease for the toe (or work a short-row toe exactly like the short-row heel).

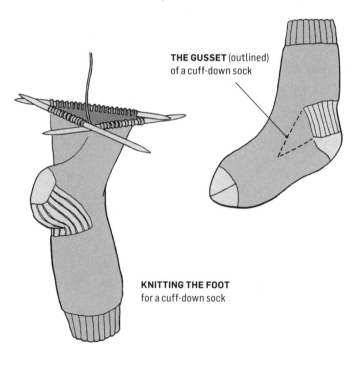

THE GUSSET (outlined) of a cuff-down sock

KNITTING THE FOOT for a cuff-down sock

Shaping the Toe and Finishing

Begin decreasing for the toe when you get just past that last knuckle on the big toe. Then, decrease 4 stitches every other round until half the stitches are used up. From there, decrease every round until you have somewhere between 4 and 16 stitches left. For more on when to begin toe shaping, see page 67.

- If the decreases are made evenly around the foot, you decrease down to 4–8 stitches, then gather them (like you do at the top of a hat or on a mitten tip).
- If the decreases are made at the side edges of the foot, you decrease down to about 16 stitches, then graft the toe with Kitchener stitch (see page 68).

When you've closed the toe, weave in any loose ends and block (see page 58).

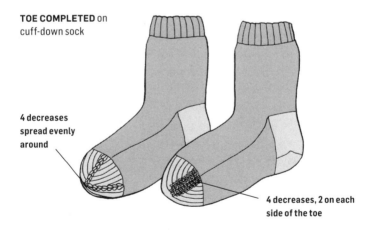

TOE COMPLETED on cuff-down sock

4 decreases spread evenly around

4 decreases, 2 on each side of the toe

Weaving in Ends

Always leave at least 4 to 6 inches of yarn as a tail when you cast on, bind off, or change yarns in a project. To weave in these ends, thread the tail of yarn onto a blunt tapestry needle. On the wrong side, weave the tail in and out of the bumps on the back of the fabric. Weave in one direction for a few inches, then turn and work in the opposite direction for about 1 inch. Then you can safely trim it close to the surface of the knitting.

Blocking Socks

You should always block a finished knitting project to relax the yarn. For socks, you can wash the socks and let them dry flat, or if you want to open up the patterns and give the socks a more finished look — especially if they're gifts — you can use sock blockers. A sock blocker is simply a piece of wood, plastic, or metal that is shaped approximately like a human foot. Just put the wet sock on the blocker and let it air dry.

BASIC CUFF-DOWN SOCK PATTERN

This pattern is written for working in k2, p2 ribbing and stockinette stitch and using sock yarn that works up at 7 stitches per inch (28 stitches per 4 inches). To customize socks for different yarn weights or pattern stitches, see page 35.

SIZES AND FINISHED MEASUREMENTS
- Child's S (Child's M, Child's L, Adult S, Adult M, Adult L, Adult XL)
- Circumference: 5½ (6½, 7, 8, 8½, 9, 9½) inches

MATERIALS
- Fingering-weight yarn: approximately 200–400 yards depending on size (see Standard Yarn Weights, page 4)
- U.S. size 3 (3.25 mm) needles for working the leg and foot in the round *or size needed to obtain gauge*
- U.S. size 1 (2.25 mm) needles for working the cuff in the round, or two sizes smaller than gauge for the leg (see page 76)
- Spare needle or stitch holder
- Stitch markers
- Tapestry needle

GAUGE
- 28 stitches = 4 inches in stockinette stitch with larger needles

ABBREVIATIONS
- For knitting abbreviations, see page 120.

(continued on next page)

CASTING ON

First, cast on for the top of the leg. Cast on loosely (use two needles held together or a larger needle) because this edge has to fit over your heel and not feel binding on your leg.

Use the loose long-tail cast on (see pages 50–51) to cast on 40 (44, 52, 56, 60, 64, 68) stitches. Take care to keep the stitches spread apart on the needle so the cast-on edge is not binding. Divide stitches into sections for double-pointed needles or circular needles. Join to work in the round, being careful not to twist the stitches.

WORKING THE CUFF

Next, work the cuff. I like to use a very stretchy ribbing like k1, p1 or k2, p2. These make the stretchiest knitted fabrics, and the cuffs will be both snug and elastic.

Work in k2, p2 ribbing for 2¼ (2¼, 3¼, 3½, 4, 4¼, 5) inches.

WORKING THE LEG

After the cuff is finished, you just knit straight down to the heel for calf-high socks. You can continue in ribbing as established or you can change to another pattern stitch for the leg of the sock (see chapter 10 for suggestions). For gifts, using a ribbing pattern is the safest bet because it's so stretchy it will fit even if your measurements or gauge are not quite right. After you get some practice, try socks with stockinette stitch, lace, or cables on the leg for added variety!

Calculating for Kneesock Shaping

If you want to make kneesocks, start with more stitches to fit over the calf, then decrease to get down to the right size at the ankle.

1. Measure your calf circumference, subtract for negative ease, and multiply by your number of stitches per inch. This is the number of stitches you need for the calf.

2. After you work the cuff, you will need to decrease from this number to the number of stitches needed for your ankle circumference. Traditionally, decreases are worked on both sides of a center back purl, or "seam," stitch.
See pages 42 and 52 for more tips on knitting kneesocks.

Continue in ribbing as set, or change to larger needles and stockinette stitch, and work even — with no increasing or decreasing — until total length measures 4½ (5½, 6½, 7, 7½, 8, 8½) inches or the desired length to the heel.

WORKING THE HEEL

My favorite heel for cuff-down socks has a heel flap and a heel turn. I like the way these look, and you can change colors of each section for a fun but easy design quirk. You can easily adjust the instep depth by making the heel flap shorter or longer. There are many different ways to work a heel flap and turn. I've used the heel stitch here, which alternates between

(continued on page 62)

slipped stitches and knits on right-side rows for a double-thick fabric, and the Dutch heel turn, which is easy to knit because the number of stitches stays the same on every row.

The heel flap is worked back and forth in heel stitch on 20 (22, 26, 28, 30, 32, 34) stitches.

Setup row 1 (RS): Knit across 10 (11, 13, 14, 15, 16, 17) stitches.

Setup row 2 (WS): Turn and purl 20 (22, 26, 28, 30, 32, 34) stitches. These are the heel flap stitches.

Place the remaining stitches on a spare needle or holder to be worked later. *Tip:* Always make note of the last row worked on the instep before you put those stitches on hold to work the heel. That way, you can start on the next row for the gusset, after the heel is turned, so your pattern stitch continues without interruption or mistakes.

Row 1 (RS): *Slip 1 purlwise with yarn in back, k1; repeat from * across.

Row 2: Slip 1 purlwise with yarn in front, then purl across.

Repeat rows 1 and 2 until flap measures 2¼ (3¼, 3¼, 4, 4¼, 4½, 4¾) inches. End after working a wrong-side row.

TURNING THE HEEL

Divide the heel into three equal sections, separated by markers. If you have an odd stitch, put it in the center section.

Row 1 (RS): Slip 1 purlwise, knit to the second marker, slip marker, ssk, turn.

Row 2: Slip 1 purlwise, purl to the second marker, p2tog, turn.

Repeat the last 2 rows until all stitches have been used.

Next row (RS): Slip 1, knit across.

Counting Heel Stitches

Note that as you turn the heel, the number of stitches in the center remains the same, and the number of stitches on the sides gets smaller and smaller.

WORKING THE GUSSET

After the heel is completed, you return to knitting in the round. You'll have live stitches that you put on hold for the instep and more live stitches at the end of the heel, but notice that there are gaps on the sides of the heel flap where there are no stitches. So the first thing you have to do is work around the entire sock and pick up stitches on the sides of the heel flap so you have a full circle of stitches again. When you work across the instep, you can continue the same pattern stitch that was established on the leg or you can change to stockinette stitch. The sole is always worked in stockinette stitch.

(continued on next page)

The sides of the gusset and the sole are always worked in stockinette stitch (because it's flat, comfortable, and easy to knit). Divide the stitches so the instep and sole stitches are in two separate sections either by using markers or by arranging the stitches as follows:

For double-pointed needles: With one double-pointed needle, knit across heel stitches. Pick up and knit 1 stitch in each slip-stitch chain along the side of the heel (see illustration, page 55). With a second double-pointed needle, work across the instep stitches (previously put on hold) in pattern. With a third double-pointed needle, pick up and knit stitches in the chains along the other side of the heel, and knit across half of the heel stitches. Place marker for the end of the round; this is the center of the bottom of the foot.

For two circular needles or Magic Loop: With one circular needle, knit across the heel stitches, then pick up and knit 1 stitch in each slip-stitch chain along the side of the heel (see illustration, page 55), place marker, and work to the center of the held instep stitches. With second circular needle or the other part of the long circular for Magic Loop, work across the second half of the instep stitches. Place marker, pick up and knit stitches in the chains along other side of the heel, and knit across the remaining unknit heel stitches. This is the center of the bottom of the foot and the beginning of the round.

Now that you're working in the round again, you have to decrease to get back to the original number of stitches so the foot circumference matches the ankle circumference on the sock. When you picked up stitches on the sides of the heel flap, you ended up with too many stitches on the sole of the sock. (The instep stitch count didn't change because those stitches were left on hold while we were knitting the heel.) Now you will decrease on both sides of the sole until all the extra stitches are gone.

Round 1: Knit to the last 3 stitches on sole, k2tog, k1. Work across instep stitches in pattern as established. On the second half of the sole stitches, k1, ssk, knit to end of round (center bottom of foot).

Round 2: Work even in pattern as established on instep and stockinette stitch on sole.

Repeat rounds 1 and 2 until 40 (44, 52, 56, 60, 64, 68) stitches remain.

WORKING THE FOOT

The rest of the foot is just a straight tube like the leg. If you didn't change to stockinette stitch, remember to keep working the pattern as established on the instep.

Work even with pattern on top of foot and stockinette stitch on sole until the piece measures 4½ (5½, 6½, 7½, 8, 8, 8½) inches from back of heel or 1¼ (1½, 1¾, 2, 2, 2¼, 2¼) inches less than desired total foot length. (See Determining Toe Length for Cuff-Down Socks, page 67.)

(continued on next page)

WORKING THE WEDGE TOE

The most popular toe on handknit socks is shaped like a wedge: flat on the top and bottom of the foot and tapered in toward a point on the two sides. Four stitches are decreased in a round, but they're not spread out evenly; instead they are worked at the two sides of the sock (on both the top and bottom) to form a shape that approximates the shape of a foot. The sock toe is symmetrical where a foot is not, but because knitting is so flexible and stretchy, this toe form fits when worn. You can adjust the length of the toe by working the decrease rows farther apart (to add length) or closer together (to make the toe shorter). The toe is worked entirely in stockinette stitch.

If you are still working ribbing (or any other pattern) on top of foot, change to stockinette stitch for the toe decreases.

Round 1 (decrease round): Knit to the last 3 stitches on the sole, k2tog, k1; on top of foot, k1, ssk, knit to the last 3 stitches, k2tog, k1; on second half of sole, k1, ssk, knit to end of round.

Round 2: Knit.

Work rounds 1 and 2 until 20 (20, 24, 28, 28, 32, 36) stitches remain, then decrease every round until 16 stitches remain.

FINISHING THE SOCK

This type of wedge toe is normally finished by grafting the stitches together using the Kitchener stitch (see page 68).

This mimics a row of stockinette stitch at the tip of the toe and is completely smooth and invisible. Another option for closing the toe that is much easier to work but not invisible (or smooth) is to simply gather in the remaining live stitches with the tail of the yarn.

Knit to the end of the needle. Break the yarn and place the sole stitches on one needle and the instep stitches on another. Graft the toe with Kitchener stitch or thread the tail through the remaining stitches, and pull gently to fasten off. Weave in ends. Wash and block as desired.

....

Determining Toe Length for Cuff-Down Socks

On a cuff-down wedge toe, 4 stitches are decreased every other round until half the stitches remain, then 4 stitches are decreased every round until between 8 and 16 stitches remain for closing the toe. To estimate the length the toe will be, subtract the number of stitches that remain from the total number of stitches you began with. The result is how many stitches you need to decrease. Divide by 4 to get the total number of decrease rounds to be worked. Take this number and multiply it by 1.5 to get the total number of rounds worked in the toe.

For example, if you have 56 stitches, you will need to decrease 40 stitches to have 16 remaining. Divide 40 stitches by 4 to find that you will have 10 decrease rounds. Multiply 10 by 1.5 to find that you will have 15 toe rounds. Multiply 15 by your row gauge to determine the length of the toe. Subtract the toe length from your foot length to determine when to stop knitting the foot.

....

Kitchener Stitch

Kitchener stitch reputedly was invented by Horatio Herbert Kitchener, 1st Earl Kitchener, during World War I. Until that time, socks typically had seamed toes that caused great discomfort for soldiers on marches and in the wet and muddy trenches and rubbed the men's toes raw, which in turn could result in dangerous infections.

To work this grafting technique, you must have the same number of stitches in each group to be joined together. Arrange your stitches on two needles, with the sole stitches on one needle and the stitches from the top of the foot on the second.

Break off the working yarn, leaving a tail about 8 or 10 inches long — long enough to work all the way across the join, with yarn left over for weaving in the end. Thread this working strand onto a tapestry needle with a blunt point.

Setup: Hold the two pieces together on the two knitting needles, wrong sides together, positioned so the working strand comes from the right-hand stitch on the front needle. Insert the tapestry needle into the first stitch on the back needle as if to knit and draw the yarn through, but don't take the stitch off the knitting needle. Then insert the tapestry needle into the first stitch on the front needle as if to purl, draw the yarn through, and, again, don't take the stitch off the needle.

Step 1. Take the tapestry needle to the back needle and insert it in the first stitch as if to purl, then remove that stitch from its needle. Insert the tapestry needle into the next stitch on the back needle as if to knit, draw the yarn through, but do not remove the stitch from the knitting needle.

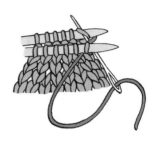

Step 2. Take the tapestry needle to the front needle and insert it in the first stitch as if to knit, draw the yarn through, then remove that stitch from the needle. Insert the tapestry needle

into the next stitch on the front needle as if to purl, draw the yarn through, but do not remove the stitch from the knitting needle.

Repeat steps 1 and 2 until one stitch remains on each needle. Follow the established pattern as well as possible with these two stitches: one will be removed from its needle after the second pass of the tapestry needle, but there will be no second stitch on that needle to go through before moving to the other needle. Enter the final stitch just once with the tapestry needle. Fasten off.

CHAPTER SEVEN

KNITTING TOE-UP SOCKS

This time, let's go through the parts of a sock knit from the toe (see chapter 4) in more detail, starting with the cast on and working our way up to the cuff. Again, this is an overview, so don't worry if some parts seem confusing. I'll go over each part in even more detail in the instructions beginning on page 77. You don't start with a "cast-on edge" because (1) there's no "edge," and (2) you may not be starting at the tip of the toe, depending on which type of toe you start with.

Two Kinds of Toes

Wedge toe. The cast on for a wedge toe in a toe-up sock is two sided; that is, you cast on just a few stitches for the tip of the toe; then you knit on both sides of the cast-on edge to work in the round. Traditional techniques are more or less based on just wrapping the yarn around the two needles, then making stitches on the first round to lock the yarn in place. These cast-on techniques are deceptively simple, but working the first round is incredibly awkward and often the tension needs to be adjusted manually before you weave in the beginning tail. A newer technique, called "Judy's Magic Cast-On" (after its "unventor," Judy Becker), is a little trickier to work but makes it much easier to knit the first round. That's the technique I recommend today, and the instructions are included on pages 98–99.

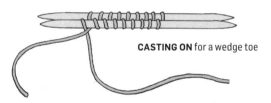

CASTING ON for a wedge toe

Because we're beginning at the tip of the toe here, shaping is accomplished by increasing, usually at both sides of the foot, with the stitches divided into sections for the bottom of the foot (the sole) and the top of the foot (the instep).

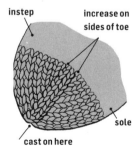

instep

increase on sides of toe

sole

cast on here

Short-row toe. Short-row toes are worked in a completely different way from wedge toes. You don't begin at the tip of the toe. Instead, you use a provisional cast on to begin where the toe meets the foot on the sole. Next, you work rows that are shorter and shorter to make a point at the tip of the toe, then rows that are longer and longer and joined to the sides of the toe bottom to create the top of the toe. When you have created a closed clamshell shape and are back to your original number of stitches, you remove the provisional cast on and begin knitting in the round for the foot. (See pages 79–82 for complete instructions on how this is done.)

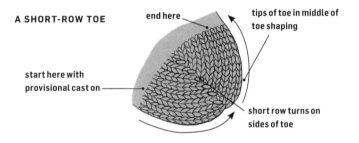

A SHORT-ROW TOE   end here

tips of toe in middle of toe shaping

start here with provisional cast on

short row turns on sides of toe

Keep It Simple

Although it is possible to make toe-up socks with gusset shaping, a heel flap, and a heel turn, it is beyond the scope of this book, and I don't recommend it for beginning sock knitters. To adjust the instep depth on a toe-up sock without a heel flap, you work the heel on fewer than half the stitches (as few as 40 percent of the total number in the sock) for a shallow instep and on more stitches (up to 60 percent) for a deep instep.

Knitting the Foot

After you've completed the toe, work even to the heel opening, which is just below the center of your ankle bone. If you want, you can put patterning on the top of the foot. If your patterning has an odd number of stitches, it's okay to divide the stitches for the top of the foot and the sole so they are not exactly the same number of stitches. The sole is always worked in plain stockinette stitch.

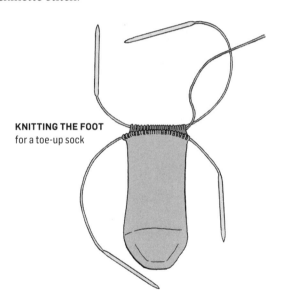

KNITTING THE FOOT
for a toe-up sock

Working the Heel

The heel on a toe-up sock is usually knit without a flap. A basic heel is worked on the sole stitches, usually half the total number of stitches in a sock, although this can be off by a few stitches to accommodate for centering patterns (see page 111) or to adjust inset depth. I usually work a short-row heel on toe-up socks.

I think of a short-row heel as a giant heel turn. You can also think of it as a clamshell: the first half of the clamshell is made by working fewer and fewer stitches in each row, and the second half of the clamshell is made by working more and more stitches in each row. In the illustration below you can see a short-row heel, with the first half of the heel complete, ready to knit the second half where the rows will get longer and longer and join to the rows from the first half.

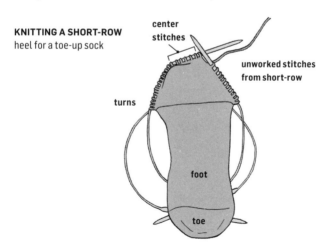

KNITTING A SHORT-ROW heel for a toe-up sock

center stitches

unworked stitches from short-row

turns

foot

toe

The short-row heel is worked exactly the same as the short-row toe, with the half of the stitches on the bottom of the foot and half on the top. (There's no need for the provisional cast on, of course, because you already have live stitches.)

Working up the Leg

On a toe-up sock, you either knit the leg straight or, for a kneesock, increase as you go up from the ankle toward the cuff (see Shaping Kneesocks, page 52).

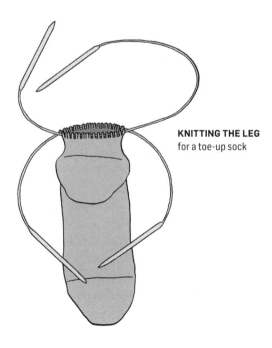

KNITTING THE LEG
for a toe-up sock

Working the Cuff, Binding Off, and Finishing

Work the cuff on smaller needles and with a ribbed stitch to ensure that it is elastic enough to stretch over the heel but snug enough to hold the sock up.

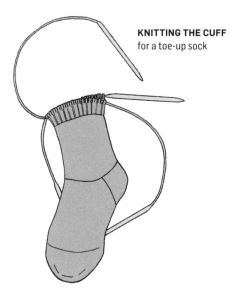

KNITTING THE CUFF
for a toe-up sock

When you bind off, *stretchy* is the key word. My favorite bind-off technique is very simple: k1, *k1, insert the left needle into the 2 stitches on the right needle and k2tog-tbl; repeat from * until all stitches are bound off. Cut the yarn and pull the tail through the last stitch to fasten off.

To finish, weave in the ends and wash the socks to relax the yarn. Block them on sock blockers, if desired (see page 58).

BASIC TOE-UP SOCK PATTERN

This pattern is written for working in k2, p2 ribbing and stockinette stitch with a short-row toe and heel, using sock yarn that works up at 7 stitches per inch. To customize socks, see page 35; for pattern stitches, see pages 112–18.

SIZES AND FINISHED MEASUREMENTS

- Child's S (Child's M, Child's L, Adult S, Adult M, Adult L, Adult XL)
- Circumference: 5½ (6½, 7, 8, 8½, 9, 9½) inches

MATERIALS

- Fingering-weight yarn: approximately 200–400 yards of yarn depending on size (see Standard Yarn Weights on page 4)
- U.S. size 3 (3.25 mm) needles for working the sock in the round *or size needed to obtain gauge*
- U.S. size 1 (2.25 mm) needles for working the top ribbing in the round or two sizes smaller than gauge needle
- Crochet hook approximately the same size as the larger needles and a few yards of fingering-weight scrap yarn for provisional cast on
- Tapestry needle

GAUGE

- 28 stitches = 4 inches in stockinette stitch with larger needles

(continued on next page)

The Provisional Cast On

1. With the scrap yarn, make a slip knot and place it on the crochet hook. Hold the crochet hook in your right hand and the knitting needle in your left hand.

2. *Take the working yarn under the knitting needle. Place the crochet hook on top of the knitting needle. Grab the working yarn with the crochet hook and crochet a chain stitch by pulling the yarn through the loop on the hook to create a stitch on the knitting needle. Repeat from * until you have the number of stitches you need.

3. Cut the yarn, and pass the tail through the loop on the crochet hook to fasten off loosely.

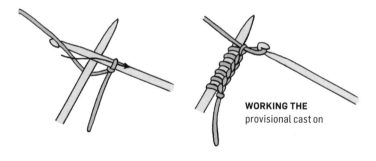

WORKING THE
provisional cast on

CASTING ON

The first thing to do on a toe-up sock is to cast on for the toe. This pattern uses a short-row toe: you will cast on half of the number of stitches you need for your foot circumference using a provisional cast-on technique so you can release the live stitches from the cast on to use for knitting in the round later.

Using a provisional cast-on technique below, cast on 20 (22, 26, 28, 30, 32, 34) stitches.

For knitting abbreviations, see page 120.

WORKING THE SHORT-ROW TOE

We'll begin by working back and forth to create the toe. Note that in the first section your rows get shorter and shorter ("short rows"); in the second section, the rows get longer and longer. This creates a clamshell-shaped toe. When the shaping is complete, you will remove the scrap yarn from the provisional cast on, place those stitches on needles, and begin knitting in the round for the foot.

Row 1 (RS): Attach working yarn, and knit to last stitch but do not knit it, turn.

Row 2 (WS): Yo, purl to last stitch but do not purl this stitch, turn.

Row 3: Yo, knit to the first knit to the stitch before the first yarnover, but do not knit this stitch (from here on, this is referred to as the "stitch/yo pair"), turn.

Row 4: Yo, purl to the first stitch/yo pair but do not purl this stitch, turn.

(continued on next page)

Repeat rows 3 and 4 until 6 (6, 8, 8, 10, 10, 12) stitches remain between the stitch/yo pairs.

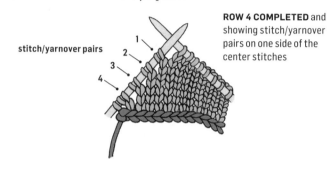

stitch/yarnover pairs

ROW 4 COMPLETED and showing stitch/yarnover pairs on one side of the center stitches

Short Rows

When you turn in the middle of the row, this is called a *short row*. To avoid a hole where you turn, you must work a special technique that adds extra yarn in this spot. I use a yarnover technique for turning in the middle of the row in this pattern. There are other short-row techniques that are also popular, and if you know one of them, feel free to substitute it here. See chapter 8 for other short-row toe and heel versions.

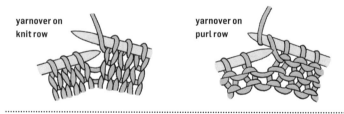

yarnover on knit row

yarnover on purl row

Next row (RS): Yo, knit to the first yo, k2tog (joining the yo and the knit stitch in the next stitch/yo pair), turn.

Next row (WS): Yo, purl to the first yo, ssp (joining the yo and the purl stitch in the next stitch/yo pair), turn.

Next row: Yo, knit to the first yo, k3tog (joining the 2 yos and the following stitch together), turn.

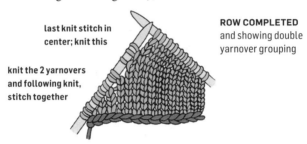

last knit stitch in center; knit this

knit the 2 yarnovers and following knit, stitch together

ROW COMPLETED and showing double yarnover grouping

Next row: Yo, purl to the first yo, sssp (joining the 2 yos and the following stitch together), turn.

Repeat the last 2 rows until the last stitch on each end is consumed, ending with a WS row.

Release the stitches from the provisional cast on starting at the end of the chain where you fastened off. Pass the end of the tail back out through the loop that secures the end of the chain to release the chain. Pulling on this loose tail carefully, try to unravel the chain one stitch at a time. As each stitch comes loose from the chain, place it on a knitting needle.

Transfer the new live stitches to two double-pointed needles or a second circular needle. The original stitches are the

(continued on next page)

instep stitches, and the new stitches are the sole stitches. Note that when you release the provisional cast on stitches, you have 1 fewer stitch than when you started, so increase after the first stitch of the second round to bring the sole stitches to the correct count: 40 (44, 52, 56, 60, 64, 68) stitches.

Joining round (RS): Working across the instep stitches, yo, knit to the remaining yo, then slip the yo to the needle holding the sole stitches and k2tog (joining the yo and the first sole stitch); knit to last sole stitch, then slip the last remaining yo on the instep needle to the needle holding the sole stitches and ssk (joining the yo and the last sole stitch). The end of the round is on the side edge of the foot.

WORKING THE FOOT

The foot is worked as a tube, with no increases or decreases until you get to the heel. You can work the entire foot in stockinette, or work ribbing (as shown below) or another pattern stitch on the instep stitches and stockinette on the sole stitches.
Knit 1 round.

Setup patterns: Knit 10 (12, 12, 14, 14, 14, 16) stitches for the sole, then continue rib across the remaining 10 (10, 14, 14, 14, 18, 18) for the top of the foot as follows: p1, (k2, p2) to last 3 stitches, k2, p1 — or center your pattern stitch on the top of the foot (see page 111).

Continue to work in pattern as established until foot measures 4½ (5½, 6½, 7½, 8, 8, 8½) inches from the tip of toe or 1¼ (1½, 1¾, 2, 2, 2¼, 2¼) inches less than the desired total foot length.

WORKING THE SHORT-ROW HEEL

The heel is worked back and forth on half of the total stitches. Fudge this as necessary to center your pattern stitch on the instep (see Centering Patterns, page 111). It's perfectly fine if you have a slightly different number of stitches in the heel and the instep. Place the instep stitches on a stitch holder or extra needle while you work the heel.

Work short rows on the heel stitches, following the steps above for Working the Short-Row Toe (page 79), beginning with Row 1 and ending just before the joining round.

Joining round (RS): If your instep stitches are on a stitch holder, place them on a needle in order to again join the stitches and work in the round. Beginning on a right-side row of the heel stitches, yo, knit to the remaining yo, then slip the yo to the needle holding the instep stitches, and knit the yo and the first instep stitch together in the established pattern. Continue in pattern across to the last instep stitch, then slip the last remaining yo from the heel needle to the instep needle and work the yo and the last instep stitch together in established pattern, using ssk.

Knit 1 round.

(continued on next page)

WORKING THE LEG

After the heel is finished, you just knit straight up to the cuff
for calf-high socks. Work the ribbing pattern — or the stitch
pattern used on the top of the foot — around the entire leg.

Continue in pattern as established on top of foot, which
is now the front of the leg, and extend the pattern over the
remaining stitches, which are now the back of the leg. Work
even until leg measures 6 inches or desired length to cuff.

WORKING THE CUFF

For the cuff, continue the same ribbing pattern as the leg,
but change to smaller needles to help hold the socks up and
continue in ribbing for 1 inch or to desired length for cuff.
Bind off (see The Stretchy Bind Off on the facing page) loosely
in pattern.

FINISHING

Weave in loose ends. Block as desired.

The Stretchy Bind Off

1. Knit 2 stitches.

2. *Insert the left needle into the front of the 2 stitches on the right needle from left to right and knit them together.

3. Knit another stitch, and repeat the process every time you have two stitches on the right needle. When all of the stitches have been bound off, cut the yarn and pull on the last stitch until the yarn comes through.

4. To close the join so you can't see where the round begins and ends, work one embroidery stitch: thread the tail onto a tapestry needle, then draw it through both sides of the bound-off stitch lying on top of the cuff at the beginning of the round.

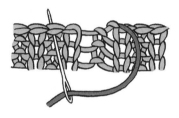

5. Insert the needle into the center of the last stitch of the round where the tail originated and pull the yarn through gently, so the new loop just formed is the same tension as the rest of the knitting in the bind off.

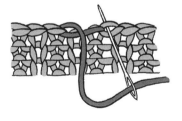

CHAPTER EIGHT

HEEL AND TOE VARIATIONS

You can substitute any of the following heel or toe techniques in any sock pattern that follows the basic constructions described in this book. Because heels are worked on half of the number of stitches used for the foot and leg circumference, it is very easy to change a pattern and use your preferred heel in almost any sock. Simply circle the heel instructions in your pattern and use the instructions for your favorite heel in their place, working with the number of stitches specified by the designer.

MORE WAYS TO WORK A HEEL

THERE ARE MANY DIFFERENT WAYS to knit sock heels. They all form a pocket at the back of the foot and turn the corner between the leg and foot of the sock. Each type of heel is shaped just a bit differently, and many knitters find that they prefer the fit of one type over another. In addition, each heel is knit with different techniques, and many knitters find that one particular heel becomes their favorite to knit.

THE FRENCH HEEL

The French heel is worked on cuff-down socks and consists of a heel flap plus a heel shaped like a trapezoid that is almost a triangle (but it does not come to a sharp point).

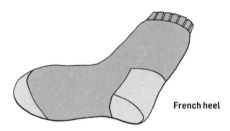

French heel

WORKING THE HEEL FLAP

Row 1 (RS): *Slip 1 purlwise, k1; repeat from * across.

Row 2 (WS): Slip 1 purlwise wyif, bring yarn to back between stitches, k2, purl across to last 3 stitches, k3.

(continued on next page)

Repeat rows 1 and 2 until heel flap is a square (as tall as it is wide) or until the heel flap is the desired length (longer for a deep instep, shorter for a shallow instep). End after working a WS row.

TURNING THE HEEL

Mark the center of the heel with a stitch marker.

Row 1 (RS): Slip 1, knit to 3 stitches past the center, removing the marker when you come to it, ssk, k1, turn.

Row 2 (WS): Slip 1, p6, p2tog, k1, turn.

Row 3: Slip 1, k7, ssk, k1, turn.

Row 4: Slip 1, p8, p2tog, k1, turn.

Continue working 1 more stitch on each row until all stitches have been worked, ending after working a WS row.

Last row (RS): Slip 1, knit across.

Changing the Heel Size

For a wider and shorter heel, you can start by working more than 3 stitches past the center. Go an equal distance past the center on row 2, then work one more stitch in each following row.

WRAP-AND-TURN SHORT-ROW HEEL

This version of a short-row heel is worked on both cuff-down and toe-up socks with the traditional wrap-and-turn short-row technique. Other than that, it is identical to the short-row heel used in the pattern on page 83. Work back and forth on sole stitches *only* as follows.

DECREASE SECTION

Row 1 (RS): Knit to 1 stitch before end of heel stitches, wrap and turn (w&t; see page 90).

Row 2 (WS): Purl to 1 stitch before end of heel stitches, w&t.

Row 3: Knit to 1 stitch before last wrapped stitch, w&t.

Row 4: Purl to 1 stitch before last wrapped stitch, w&t.

Continue as established, working always to one stitch before the last wrapped stitch. Work until about a third of the stitches remain unwrapped in the center, ending with a WS row.

INCREASE SECTION

Row 1: Knit to first wrapped stitch, knit it (working the wrap with the stitch), w&t. (*Note:* Since the next stitch has already been wrapped, you are creating a double-wrapped stitch.)

Row 2: Purl to first wrapped stitch, purl wrapped stitch, w&t.

Row 3: Knit to first double-wrapped stitch, knit it (working both wraps with the stitch), w&t.

(continued on next page)

Row 4: Purl to first double-wrapped stitch, purl it, w&t (wrap and turn; see below).

Continue as established, always working the wraps of the wrapped stitches with the stitch itself, until all the stitches of the heel have been worked and you're back to the number you started with.

....

Wrap and Turn (W&T)

1. Work to the turning point.

2. Slip the next stitch onto the right needle purlwise.

3. Bring the yarn to the front (on a knit row) or back (on a purl row), then move the same stitch back to the left needle.

4. Turn the work, bring the yarn to front or back as needed to knit or purl the next stitch and work across the following row.

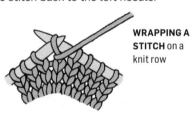

WRAPPING A STITCH on a knit row

This wrap-and-turn technique creates a float on the right side of the work. On the next complete row, you will work back over the wrapped stitch. Knit the wrap together with the corresponding stitch on the left needle to close up the holes created by the short-row shaping.

....

GERMAN DOUBLE-STITCH SHORT-ROW HEEL

This version of a short-row heel, worked on both cuff-down and toe-up socks with a German short-row technique, is called a *double stitch*. In addition, there are two plain rounds of knitting in the center of the heel that add a bit of extra depth to the instep. Work back and forth on sole stitches *only* as follows.

DECREASE SECTION

Row 1 (RS): Knit across; turn.

Row 2 (WS): Make a double stitch as follows: Slip the first stitch purlwise with yarn in front, then pull the working yarn up over the top of the needle to the back as tightly as you can to draw both legs of the slipped stitch up over the right needle so it looks like you have two stitches. Bring the yarn between the needles to the front and purl across. Turn.

MAKING A
double stitch

Row 3: Make a double stitch (as in row 2), then knit across to the first double stitch at the other end. Do not work the double stitch. Turn.

Row 4: Make a double stitch, then purl across to the first double stitch at the other end. Do not work the double stitch. Turn.

(continued on next page)

Repeat rows 3 and 4 until about one-third of the original stitches remain in the center between double stitches. End after working a WS row. Slip a marker on the needle at each side of the center stitches to mark them.

CENTER SECTION

Beginning at the start of RS row of the heel, work 2 rounds — going all the way around the leg — with no shaping, working both loops of each double stitch together as 1 stitch. Remember to work the stitches on top of the leg following the next row of pattern as established. End at the beginning of the heel stitches.

INCREASE SECTION

You finish turning the heel by working your double stitches in reverse and working back out to the edge of the heel on the side panels (double stitches), as follows:

Row 1 (RS): Knit to second marker, remove marker, k1; turn.

Row 2 (WS): Make a double stitch in the first stitch of the side panel, purl to the remaining marker, remove marker, p1; turn.

Row 3: Make a double stitch, knit to the first double stitch at the other end, knit both loops of the double stitch together as 1 stitch, k1; turn.

Row 4: Make a double stitch, purl to the first double stitch on the other end, purl both loops of the double stitch together as 1 stitch, p1; turn.

Repeat rows 3 and 4 until all your side panel stitches are added back in as regular stitches.

Return to work in the round on all stitches.

AFTERTHOUGHT HEEL

An afterthought heel (sometimes referred to as a peasant heel) is made after the cuff-down or the toe-up sock is complete. You leave a hole in the knitting, either by knitting the heel stitches with scrap yarn and removing it later, or by putting the heel stitches on a stitch holder and doing a provisional cast on (see page 78) above the opening. You then pick up those stitches later to knit the heel, using decreases for shaping. The afterthought heel also is the easiest to replace on a sock.

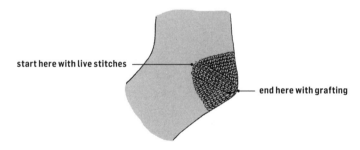

start here with live stitches

end here with grafting

PREPARING THE HEEL OPENING

At the point where you want to begin the heel, work across the sole stitches in scrap yarn. Slip these stitches back to the left-hand needle, and knit them again with the working yarn.

(continued on next page)

Continue knitting the rest of the sock. After completing the sock, come back to work the heel.

KNITTING THE HEEL

Remove the scrap yarn, and put the heel stitches onto three or four (as desired) double-pointed needles (or on two circular needles). The stitches for the bottom of the heel should be on two double-pointed needles (or the first circular needle), and the stitches for the back of the leg should be on another one or two double-pointed needles (or the second circular).

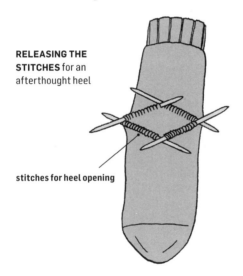

RELEASING THE STITCHES for an afterthought heel

stitches for heel opening

Work carefully, releasing the stitches one by one and putting them on their new needles as you do so. The end of the round is at the side edge between the bottom of the heel and the back of the heel.

Knit 3 rounds.

Decrease round: *K1, ssk, knit to the last 3 stitches on the bottom of the heel, k2tog, k1; repeat from * on the back of the heel.

Next round: Knit.

Repeat the last 2 rounds until one-third of the heel stitches remain or, for a shorter, wider heel, switch to decreasing every round when about half your stitches remain. Arrange the stitches so the remaining sole stitches are on one needle and the stitches at the back of the heel are on a second needle.

Graft the remaining heel stitches together with Kitchener stitch (see page 68). Weave in the ends, closing up any small holes at the corners of the heel if necessary.

MORE WAYS TO WORK TOES

ON CUFF-DOWN SOCKS, toes are shaped with decreases. There are many different ways to arrange the decreases, and each one results in a different toe shape. In addition to the variety of shapes that can be made, some toes are finished off by grafting with Kitchener stitch (see page 68), while others are finished by simply gathering in the remaining stitches.

ROUND TOE

This toe technique, which can be used for both toe-up and top-down socks, eliminates the need for working Kitchener stitch to graft the final stitches together at the tip of the toe. It is an older technique that was used in many cuff-down socks before Kitchener stitch was invented. The instructions below are for working the round toe on cuff-down socks; for how to adapt the technique to toe-up socks, see Toe-Up Variation on the facing page.

Setup: Work the foot until it measures to the joint on your big toe, or until the sock is about 1 inch (for children's sizes) or 2 inches (for adults' sizes) less than your final target measurement for the foot. Divide stitches into four equal sections.

Decrease Round 1 (right sock): *Knit to the last 2 stitches in section, k2tog; repeat from * three more times.

Decrease Round 1 (left sock): *Ssk, knit to next section; repeat from * three more times.

Round 2: Knit.

Repeat rounds 1 and 2 until half of the stitches remain, then repeat round 1 until 10 or fewer stitches remain. (For a longer toe, decrease every other row more times. For a shorter toe, change to decreasing every row sooner.) Cut yarn, leaving a 6-inch tail. Thread tail through all remaining stitches, pull gently to close, then secure the tail to the inside.

....

Toe-Up Variation

To work a round toe on a toe-up sock, begin the sock with a provisional cast on (see page 78) and the full number of stitches needed for the foot. Knit the sock, release the provisional cast on, put the live stitches on the needles, and work as for a cuff-down sock. Any cuff-down toe shaped by decreases can be added to a toe-up sock as an "afterthought toe" in this fashion. The toe on a child's sock will be about 1 inch long, and the toe on an adult's sock will be about 2 inches long. (For a longer toe, decrease every other row more times. For a shorter toe, change to decreasing every row sooner.)

....

Judy's Magic Cast-On

1. Make a slip knot, leaving a tail 4 to 6 inches long for weaving in later. Place the loop, which counts as the first stitch, on a needle. Hold two needles together, with the needle that the yarn is attached to at the top. In your other hand, hold the yarn with the tail over your index finger and the working yarn over your thumb. Hold both yarns behind the bottom needle.

2. With your index finger, bring the yarn around the bottom needle from back to front, then bring the yarn between the two needles from front to back — one stitch is cast on the bottom needle.

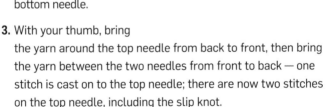

3. With your thumb, bring the yarn around the top needle from back to front, then bring the yarn between the two needles from front to back — one stitch is cast on to the top needle; there are now two stitches on the top needle, including the slip knot.

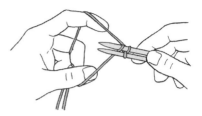

Tip: The top yarn (on the index finger) always wraps around the bottom needle, and the bottom yarn (on the thumb) always wraps around the top needle.

4. Continue alternating between steps 2 and 3 until you have the desired number of stitches. End when you have the same number of stitches on each needle after working a stitch on the bottom needle.

To begin knitting, rotate the needles 180 degrees so the working yarn is on the right-hand side. The needle formerly on the bottom is now on top, and the working yarn is attached to what is the new bottom needle.

Use a third needle to knit the row of stitches on the top needle. You will see a row of stitches appear between the two needles. Rotate the work 180 degrees, adjust your needles as necessary, and knit across the stitches on the second needle (knit these stitches *through the back loop for round 1 only*). You have now completed one full round of knitting.

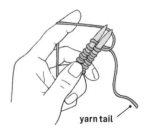

yarn tail

Divide the stitches in the round for the type of needles you are using, and continue knitting.

WEDGE TOE FOR THE TOE-UP SOCK

This is the same shape as the cuff-down wedge toe (see page 66), but it is worked in the opposite direction with increases for shaping. It begins with a bidirectional cast on that allows you to begin working in the round immediately.

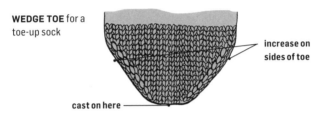

WEDGE TOE for a toe-up sock

increase on sides of toe

cast on here

Setup: With main color and using Judy's Magic Cast-On (see pages 98–99), cast on enough wraps to measure approximately 1 inch. The first half of the stitches become the top of the foot, and the second half of the stitches will be the sole.

Knit 1 round.

Next round: *K1, M1, knit to the last of the top-of-the-foot stitches, M1, k1; repeat from * on the sole stitches — 4 stitches increased.

Next round: Knit.

Divide stitches evenly on four double-pointed, two circular needles, or two sections of a long circular for Magic Loop. Use a marker or the division between needles to identify the halfway point.

Repeat the last 2 rounds until you have the total number of stitches required for your sock.

If you need to adjust the stitch count to get the correct multiple for your stitch pattern, work one more round, increasing as needed to obtain your stitch multiple.

MOCCASIN TOE FOR TOE-UP SOCKS

This toe is rounder than a wedge toe and has more depth to it. It is an excellent choice for making slipper socks or comfortable socks to wear in hiking or work boots. It can be a little too loose to fit properly in dress shoes. You can use double-pointed needles or one of the circular needle arrangements to work the moccasin toe. (It is easier to use five, rather than four, double-pointed needles for this method.)

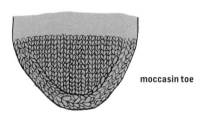

moccasin toe

1. Using the provisional cast on (see page 78), cast on 6 stitches. Fasten off.

2. Change to working yarn, and work 8 rows in stockinette stitch, beginning with a purl row.

(continued on next page)

3. Remove the provisional cast on and put the 6 stitches onto a second needle. (You will have 5 loops when you remove the provisional cast on; pick up the 6th stitch on the side edge of the piece.) Hold the piece so that the needle holding the newly released stitches is at the top and the needle holding the live stitches is at the bottom, with the working yarn at the right. Use an empty needle and the working yarn to pick up and knit 6 stitches on the side of the rectangle. With another needle, knit across the newly released stitches on the top needle. With a fourth needle, pick up 6 stitches on the other side of the rectangle. The live and provisional stitches are for the sides of the foot; the picked-up stitches on one side of the rectangle are for the sole and those on the other side are for the instep — 24 stitches.

Note: If using circular needles, *work live stitches on needle, place marker, and pick up side stitches on the same needle; repeat from * with the newly released provisional stitches on the second needle or second portion of long circular for Magic Loop.

4. Knit 1 round.

5. *Knit the side stitches; on the instep M1, knit across instep stitches, M1; repeat from * once more, knitting across the second side, then increasing at each end of the needle holding the sole stitches — 4 stitches increased.

6. Knit 1 more round.

Repeat steps 5 and 6 until you have the number of stitches required for your sock.

If you are working a pattern stitch that's not a multiple of 4, work one more round, increasing evenly around to adjust for the number of stitches for your repeat.

....

More Toe Variations: Wrap-and-Turn and German Double-Stitch Short-Row Toes

Any short-row heel can also be used as a toe. I love this, because it means that my heels and toes can match exactly! This can be worked as for heels in both cuff-down and toe-up socks (see pages 89–93) with these exceptions:

- To begin on toe-up socks, use a provisional cast on (page 78), and cast on half the number of stitches needed for your sock.
- To begin on cuff-down socks, work on the sole stitches only.
- To end on toe-up socks, release the provisional cast on, place the newly released stitches on a needle, and begin working in the round.
- To end on cuff-down socks, join with Kitchener stitch (page 68).

....

CHAPTER NINE

KNITTING TWO SOCKS AT ONCE

If you are knitting on two circulars (see page 19) or using the Magic Loop technique (see page 21), you can knit two socks at the same time, which ensures that both socks come out exactly the same. You can work both cuff-down and toe-up socks two at a time. If you are working toe-up socks, you can work until you use up every single inch of your precious yarn!

Start by casting on for one sock (one half of the stitches are in one section, and the other half are in the second section), and work a few rounds. Then put those stitches on hold, and begin the second sock in the same manner with a separate ball of yarn.

Carefully transfer the first sock back onto one or two circular needles, making sure that the working yarn is on the back needle or section so both socks are in the same orientation. You now have two socks, each attached to its own ball of yarn, on the same needles.

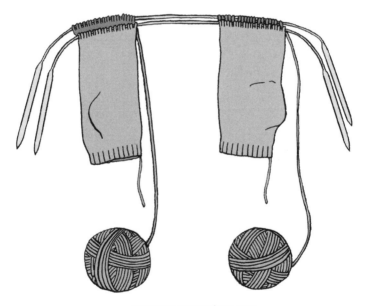

KNITTING TWO socks at once

To knit a round, work the first half of the first sock, and drop the yarn attached to that sock. Then slide the stitches of the second sock up to the left needle tip, pick up the next ball of yarn, and work the first part of the second sock.

Carefully turn the needles clockwise so that the working balls of yarn are again on the back needle, and work across the second side of each sock — each with its own ball of yarn — as above. At the end of this section, turn the needles counterclockwise so your yarns don't get twisted.

When you get to the heel, simply work back and forth over the heel stitches as you would for any needle arrangement, turning back and forth to work right-side and wrong-side rows and switching balls of yarn for each sock. Leave the instep stitches on the second needle or section of needle unworked until the heel is finished.

Keeping It Straight

You may find that keeping one ball of yarn on your left and the other on your right while knitting helps you remember to turn clockwise after the first half of the round, then counterclockwise after the second half of the round, and to keep the yarns untangled.

CHAPTER TEN

STITCH LIBRARY

The stitch options for knitting socks are almost limitless, but I've included 10 easy ribbing stitch patterns here. These all work well for stretchy socks, from simple to decorative. Each pattern stitch includes instructions for working around the whole leg, and for centering the pattern when working on the top of the foot (see page 111). Remember, however, you can always make a sock with plain stockinette stitch on the entire foot even if there is fancy patterning on the leg.

When working ribbing on the leg of a sock, work the full repeat all the way around. When working ribbing on the top of the foot, center the stitches so the pattern is the same on both sides of the instep. You can arrange this in any way you like. On the next page, you will find the options I use most often.

- For a toe-up sock, center the pattern on the instep right after you complete the toe, then switch to working the pattern around the whole leg after working the heel.
- For a cuff-down sock, establish the pattern in the round on the leg after you cast on or after working the cuff, then switch to working the pattern on only the instep after you work the heel. You must decide how to center the pattern before you begin the heel. If you wish to work the foot plain, you can change to stockinette stitch 1 inch before you begin the heel or immediately after working the heel.

More Reasons to Swatch

In addition to the reasons described in chapter 3 for working gauge swatches before you begin any sock pattern (see pages 30–33), there are other advantages for working them when you are working stitch patterns.

- You can check that the fabric texture is appropriate for the project you are making. Are your stitches too loose and sloppy looking? Is the fabric too tight and stiff? For socks, it's especially important to confirm that the fabric has elasticity and stretches enough for the sock to be comfortable.

- You can learn how to work the pattern stitch before you make a mistake on your actual sock. Practice makes perfect, and if you don't swatch, you're not practicing.

- You can also swatch to practice a technique, such as a sock heel or toe, rather than just practicing a pattern stitch on a straight tube.

K1, P1 RIBBING

To work on the leg over an even number of stitches:

All rounds: (K1, p1) around.

To work on the top of the foot over an odd number of stitches:

All rounds: (K1, p1) across top of foot, k1; work stockinette stitch across the sole.

or

All rounds: (P1, k1) across top of foot, p1; work stockinette stitch across sole.

K1, p1 ribbing

K2, P2 RIBBING

To work on the leg over a multiple of 4 stitches:

All rounds: (K2, p2) around.

To work on the top of the foot over a multiple of 4 + 2 stitches:

All rounds: (K2, p2) across to last 2 stitches on top of foot, k2; work stockinette stitch across sole.

or

All rounds: (P2, k2) across to last 2 stitches on top of foot, p2; work stockinette stitch across sole.

K2, p2 ribbing

RICKRACK RIBBING

To work on the leg over a multiple of 3 stitches:

Round 1: *P1, k-tbl of the 2nd stitch on the left needle, knit the first stitch normally, then drop them both from the needle at the same time; repeat from * around.

Round 2: *P1, knit the 2nd stitch on the left needle, then knit the first stitch, and drop them both from the needle at the same time; repeat from * around.

Repeat rounds 1 and 2 for pattern.

To work on the top of the foot over a multiple of 3 + 1 stitches:

Round 1: *P1, k-tbl of the 2nd stitch on the left needle, knit the first stitch normally, then drop them both from the needle at the same time; repeat from * to the last stitch on instep, p1; work across sole in stockinette stitch.

Round 2: *P1, knit the 2nd stitch on the left needle, then knit the first stitch and drop them both from the needle at the same time; repeat from * to the last stitch on instep, p1; work across sole in stockinette stitch.

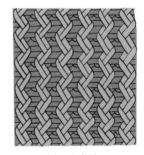

rickrack ribbing

Repeat rounds 1 and 2 for pattern.

Centering Patterns

Some patterns have one or more extra stitches on one edge that allows the pattern to be centered on flat knitting. When you see a reference to a "multiple of X stitches + X," the latter part refers to these centering stitches. This is also how you center the pattern on the top of the sock foot. Even though you are working in the round, you are not working the pattern stitch all the way around, and unless it is a very small and simple texture stitch, chances are it will look better if centered.

When working the pattern around the leg of a sock, the centering stitches are ignored.

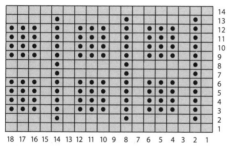

CENTERING A PATTERN
for the top of the foot

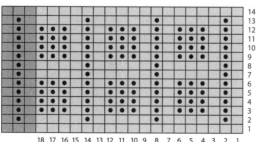

Rounding Stitch Counts to Fit

You can adjust the number of stitches in the sock patterns in this book to accommodate the multiple used in each stitch pattern in chapter 10. If you adjust only a few stitches, it won't be noticeable. For cuff-down socks, change the cast on to the number of stitches you need for your pattern or increase to this number in a plain round after the cuff. For toe-up socks, increase to this number of stitches in a plain round after the toe is complete.

For example, if you are working with a stitch pattern that has a 5-stitch repeat, you need a total number of stitches that is a multiple of 5, such as 20, 25, or 30. If the pattern in your size calls for 22 stitches, you have to round down to 20 or up to 25.

TWISTED RIBBING

To work on the leg over an even number of stitches:

All rounds: (K1-tbl, p1) around.

To work on the top of the foot over an odd number of stitches:

All rounds: (K1-tbl, p1) across top of foot to the last stitch, k1-tbl; work stockinette stitch across sole.

or

All rounds: (P1, k1-tbl) across top of foot to the last stitch, p1; work stockinette stitch across sole.

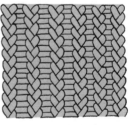

twisted ribbing

WIDE LACE RIBBING

To work on the leg over a multiple of 7 stitches:

Rounds 1, 2, and 4: (K5, p2) around.

Round 3: (K2tog, yo, k1, yo, ssk, p2) around.

Repeat rounds 1–4 for pattern.

To work on the top of the foot over a multiple of 7 + 2 stitches:

Rounds 1, 2, and 4: P2, (K5, p2) to end of instep stitches; work stockinette stitch across sole.

Round 3: P2, (K2tog, yo, k1, yo, ssk, p2) to end of instep stitches; work stockinette stitch across sole.

Repeat rounds 1–4 for pattern.

wide lace ribbing

NARROW LACE RIBBING

To work on the leg over a multiple of 6 stitches:

Rounds 1 and 3: (K2, p1) around.

Round 2: (K2, p1, yo, ssk, p1) around.

Round 4: (K2, p1, k2tog, yo, p1) around.

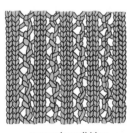

Repeat rounds 1–4 for pattern.

To work on the top of the foot over a multiple of 6 + 1 stitches:

Rounds 1 and 3: P1, (k2, p1) around.

narrow lace ribbing

(continued on next page)

Round 2: P1, (k2, p1, yo, ssk, p1) around.

Round 4: P1, (k2, p1, k2tog, yo, p1) around.

Repeat rounds 1–4 for pattern.

FOLDED RIBBON RIBBING

To work on the leg over a multiple of 9 stitches:

Round 1 and all odd-number rounds: *K6, p3; repeat from * around.

Round 2: *Yo, ssk, k4, p3; repeat from * around.

Round 4: *Yo, k1, ssk, k3, p3; repeat from * around.

Round 6: *Yo, k2, ssk, k2, p3; repeat from * around.

Round 8: *Yo, k3, ssk, k1, p3; repeat from * around.

Round 10: *Yo, k4, ssk, p3; repeat from * around.

Round 12: *K4, k2tog, yo, p3; repeat from * around.

Round 14: *K3, k2tog, k1, yo, p3; repeat from * around.

Round 16: *K2, k2tog, k2, yo, p3; repeat from * around.

Round 18: *K1, k2tog, k3, yo, p3; repeat from * around.

Round 20: *K2tog, k4, yo, p3; repeat from * around.

Repeat rounds 1–20 for pattern.

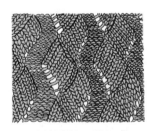

folded ribbon ribbing

To work on the top of the foot over a multiple of 9 + 3 stitches:

Round 1 and all odd-number rounds: P3, *k6, p3; repeat from * around.

Round 2: P3, *yo, ssk, k4, p3; repeat from * around.

Round 4: P3, *yo, k1, ssk, k3, p3; repeat from * around.

Round 6: P3, *yo, k2, ssk, k2, p3; repeat from * around.

Round 8: P3, *yo, k3, ssk, k1, p3; repeat from * around.

Round 10: P3, *yo, k4, ssk, p3; repeat from * around.

Round 12: P3, *k4, k2tog, yo, p3; repeat from * around.

Round 14: P3, *k3, k2tog, k1, yo, p3; repeat from * around.

Round 16: P3, *k2, k2tog, k2, yo, p3; repeat from * around.

Round 18: P3, *k1, k2tog, k3, yo, p3; repeat from * around.

Round 20: P3, *k2tog, k4, yo, p3; repeat from * around.

Repeat rounds 1–20 for pattern.

COCOON STITCH RIBBING

- **Special abbreviation — s3k2p:** Slip 3 stitches together as if to knit 3 together, k2tog, pass the 3 slipped stitches over — 5 stitches decreased to 1 stitch.

To work on the leg over a multiple of 8 stitches:

Rounds 1 and 2: *K1, p1, k1, p5; repeat from * around.

Round 3: *K1, p1 under the running thread between the stitch just worked and the next stitch, (p1, k1, p1) in the next stitch, p1 under running thread, k1, s3k2p; repeat from * around.

(continued on next page)

Rounds 4–8: *K1, p5, k1, p1; repeat from * around.

Round 9: *K1, s3k2p, k1, p1 under running thread, (p1, k1, p1) in next stitch, p1 under running thread; repeat from * around.

Rounds 10–12: Work as round 1.

Repeat rounds 1–12 for pattern.

To work on the top of the foot over a multiple of 8 + 3 stitches:

Note: Count your stitches after round 1 as stitch count varies.

Rounds 1 and 2: *K1, p1, k1, p5; repeat from * to last 3 stitches, k1, p1, k1.

Round 3: *K1, p1 under the running thread between the stitch just worked and the next stitch, (p1, k1, p1) in the next stitch, p1 under running thread, k1, s3k2p; repeat from * to the last 3 stitches, k1, p1 under the running thread between the stitch just worked and the next stitch, (p1, k1, p1) in the next stitch, p1 under running thread, k1.

Rounds 4–8: *K1, p5, k1, p1; repeat from * to the last 7 stitches, k1, p5, k1.

Round 9: *K1, s3k2p, k1, p1 under running thread, (p1, k1, p1) in next stitch, p1 under running thread, k1; repeat from * to last 7 stitches, k1, s3k2p, k1.

cocoon stitch ribbing

Rounds 10–12: Work as round 1.

Repeat rounds 1–12 for pattern.

HONEYCOMB EYELET RIBBING

To work on the leg over a multiple of 5 stitches:

Rounds 1, 2, and 4: (K3, p2) around.

Round 3: *Pass the 3rd stitch on the left needle over the first 2 stitches and drop it off the needles, k1, yo, k1, p2; repeat from * around.

Repeat rounds 1–4 for pattern.

To work on the top of the foot over a multiple of 5 + 2 stitches:

Rounds 1, 2, and 4: P2, (k3, p2) to last stitch on instep; work sole in stockinette stitch.

Round 3: P2, *pass the 3rd stitch on the left needle over the first 2 stitches and drop it off the needles, k1, yo, k1, p2; repeat from * to last stitch on instep; work sole in stockinette stitch.

Repeat rounds 1–4 for pattern.

honeycomb eyelet ribbing

TWISTED ROPE CABLE RIBBING

To work on the leg over a multiple of 5 stitches:

Rounds 1, 2, and 4: (K1-tbl, p1, k1-tbl, p2) around.

Round 3: *Slip next 2 stitches to cable needle and hold in front, k1-tbl, then slip the purl stitch back to left needle and purl it; then k1-tbl from cable needle, p2; repeat from * around.

Repeat rounds 1–4 for pattern.

To work on the top of the foot over a multiple of 5 + 2 stitches:

Rounds 1, 2, and 4: P2, *k1-tbl, p1, k1-tbl, p2; repeat from * to end of instep; work sole in stockinette stitch.

Round 3: P2, *slip next 2 stitches to cable needle and hold in front, k1-tbl, then slip the purl stitch back to left-hand needle and purl it; then k1-tbl from cable needle, p2; repeat from * to last stitch on instep; work sole in stockinette stitch.

Repeat rounds 1–4 for pattern.

twisted rope cable ribbing

MY FAVORITE KNITTING RESOURCES

Every knitter has her favorite supplies and tools. Here are some of mine.

YARNS

Fiber Arts Socks That Rock

Hillesvåg Hifa 2 Yarn

Knit Picks Stroll Sock Yarn

Koigu PPPM

Lorna's Laces Shepherd Sock

Madeline Tosh Tosh Sock

ModeKnit Yarn ModeSock

Regia 4-Ply Sock Yarn

BIBLIOGRAPHY

Budd, Ann. *Sock Knitting Master Class: Innovative Techniques + Patterns from Top Designers.* Loveland, Colo.: Interweave, 2011.

Bush, Nancy. *Folk Socks: The History & Techniques of Handknitted Footwear.* Loveland, Colo.: Interweave, revised edition 2012.

Gibson-Roberts, Priscilla. *Ethnic Socks & Stockings: A Compendium of Eastern Design & Technique.* Sioux Falls, S. Dak.: XRX Books, 1995.

Neel, Lara. *Sock Architecture: Heels, Toes, & Techniques for Knitting Awesome Socks.* Lakewood, Ohio: Cooperative Press, 2014.

ABBREVIATIONS

ABBREV.	DESCRIPTION
*	repeat instructions following the asterisk as directed
k	knit
k2tog	knit 2 stitches together
k3tog	knit 3 stitches together
kfb	knit in the front and back of the same stitch to increase
M1	make 1 (Insert the left needle under the bar between the next 2 stitches from front to back, then knit this loop through the back.)
p	purl
p2tog	purl 2 stitches together
RS	right side
ssk	slip slip knit [(Slip 1 knitwise) twice, insert the left needle into the front of the 2 slipped stitches and knit them together.]
ssp	slip slip purl [(Slip 1 knitwise) twice, put the stitches back onto the left needle (a), insert the right needle into both stitches together in the back from left to right, and purl them together (b).]
sssp	slip slip slip purl [(Slip 1 knitwise) three times, put the stitches back onto the left needle, insert the right needle into both stitches together in the back from left to right, and purl them all together.]
tbl	through the back loop
w&t	wrap and turn
WS	wrong side
wyif	with yarn in front
yo	yarnover

Metric Conversion Chart

WHEN THE MEASUREMENT GIVEN IS	TO CONVERT IT TO	MULTIPLY INCHES BY
inches	millimeters	25.40
inches	centimeters	2.54

US (INCHES)	METRIC (CENTIMETERS)	US (INCHES)	METRIC (CENTIMETERS)
⅛	3.18 mm	6	15.24
¼	6.35 mm	6½	16.51
⅜	9.53 mm	7	17.78
½	1.27	7½	19.05
⅝	1.59	8	20.32
¾	1.91	8½	21.59
⅞	2.22	9	22.86
1	2.54	9½	24.13
1½	3.81	10	25.40
2	5.08	11	27.94
2½	6.35	12	30.48
3	7.62	13	33.02
3½	8.89	14	35.56
4	10.16	15	38.10
4½	11.43		
5	12.70		
5½	13.97		

INDEX

Page numbers in *italic* indicate illustrations; page numbers in **bold** indicate tables or charts.